DEVELOPING AN OUTSTANDING CORE COLLECTION

A GUIDE FOR LIBRARIES | SECOND EDITION

CAROL ALABASTER

AMERICAN LIBRARY ASSOCIATION
CHICAGO   2010

D0249621

Carol Alabaster is one of those "women who love books too much," but an extremely fortunate one who has been able to indulge her passion full time as a librarian. She has more than thirty years' experience working for public library systems in both New York City and Phoenix. During the thirteen years she was collection development coordinator for the Phoenix Public Library, she developed and implemented systemwide core collections. In addition to writing a weekly book review for the *Arizona Republic* for more than seven years, she was a National Book Award judge in 1982. She is retired from the Phoenix Public Library but continues to foster her love for books as a book club leader and a full-time reader.

While extensive effort has gone into ensuring the reliability of information appearing in this book, the publisher makes no warranty, express or implied, on the accuracy or reliability of the information, and does not assume and hereby disclaims any liability to any person for any loss or damage caused by errors or omissions in this publication.

The paper used in this publication meets the minimum requirements of American National Standard for Information Sciences—Permanence of Paper for Printed Library Materials, ANSI Z39.48-1992. ∞

Library of Congress Cataloging-in-Publication Data
Alabaster, Carol.
   Developing an outstanding core collection : a guide for libraries / Carol Alabaster. — 2nd ed.
      p. cm.
   Includes bibliographical references and index.
   ISBN 978-0-8389-1040-5 (alk. paper)
   1. Public libraries—Collection development—United States. I. Title.
Z687.2.U6A43 2010
025.2'187473—dc22

                                                                2009040342

ISBN-13: 978-0-8389-1040-5

Printed in the United States of America
14 13 12 11 10   5 4 3 2 1

For Ralph M. Edwards, former city librarian
of the Phoenix Public Library, and for
the excellent selectors in libraries everywhere

In memory of Richard Tirotta, bibliographic specialist
at the New York Public Library for over thirty years,
the most excellent selector of us all

CONTENTS

PREFACE TO THE FIRST EDITION

*Some books are undeservedly forgotten;
none are undeservedly remembered.*
—W. H. Auden

CREATING AN ADULT CORE collection for a public library is an extremely complex and challenging endeavor. The underlying premise of a core collection is that certain books and films are standard classic titles that are at the very heart of a library's collection and form the foundation upon which a library's collection is built. *Developing an Outstanding Core Collection* is a philosophical, albeit practical, exploration of the importance of this collection nucleus. This book is a how-to guide to developing an adult core collection—a collection that opens the door to the endless possibilities inherent in books and reading.

The impetus to write this book came from my thirteen-plus years as collection development coordinator at the Phoenix Public Library. Under the direction of the city librarian, Dr. Ralph M. Edwards, collection development was the number-one priority. It was wonderfully rewarding to work full-time to transform the rambling, undefined collections of the Phoenix Public Library branches and Central Library into exemplary collections—collections that could meet the reading and information needs of the diverse citizens of one of the fastest-growing cities in the nation. It was a dream come true.

A lot of work was demanded of every librarian systemwide. The creation of the core collection was the means to lift the library from its collection doldrums. During the 1970s, the city of Phoenix had grown and left its library behind in the desert dust. Today the Phoenix Public Library is a world-class library system with an award-winning Central Library and showcase branches throughout the city. Although core collection work is no longer a priority, the seeds that were sown almost twenty years ago have germinated and grown into an amazing library system of which staff and the citizens of Phoenix can be proud.

Many longtime friends and colleagues have encouraged and helped me in writing this book. I am most grateful to the following wise and patient women, who always took time from their busy lives to read the manuscript and offer constructive suggestions: Ellen Altman, Cathy Chung, Jeanette Jenkins, Susan Jones, Susie Matazzoni, Rowena McDade, Sheila Miller, and Janice Russell. Additionally, my sincerest appreciation goes to Sandy Liberman, whose expertise, sense of humor, and ongoing encouragement greatly influenced the writing of this book.

A special thank you goes to my husband and son, who were always available when I needed them and were willing and able to help whenever my computer skills failed me.

Finally, I dedicate this book to Dr. Ralph M. Edwards, the former city librarian of the Phoenix Public Library, and in memory of Richard Tirotta, bibliographic specialist at the New York Public Library, two "book advocates" and true lovers of the printed word.

PREFACE TO THE SECOND EDITION

Today a reader, tomorrow a leader.
— Margaret Fuller

ASKED TO REVISE *Developing an Outstanding Core Collection* after almost a decade, I worried whether the core principles of my book were still valid. Was there still a place in libraries for a core collection? Were people still reading the classics? Would these titles still be considered timeless? Had the Internet truly turned readers into viewers with short attention spans, or worse yet eliminated reading completely? All my fears turned out to be unfounded.

The digital age with its access to unfathomable bytes of information, along with the increasing availability of the e-book, has certainly changed the nature of books and how we get our information. But I have no doubt that reading is alive and well. I believe that there is an even greater need today for libraries to stock books and films of the highest quality and readability and, most important, to provide guidance to our users in finding them. I look to the proliferation of "1001" compilations of the best books, the best films, the places you must see, restaurants to sample, and I find that people are looking for guidance in spending their limited time and resources. I see that book clubs are flourishing and that stores such as Target, Costco, Barnes and Noble, and Amazon are all touting their own "book club" selections, increasing sales and developing a clientele of steady readers. I take heart that President Obama, our most techno-savvy president to date, talks often about the books that made him who he is today and keeps us up on what he is currently reading. I am pleased that Big Read programs are on the rise throughout our communities. These all help explain why for the first time in over twenty-five years the National Endowment for the Arts reports that the decline in adult reading in our country has reversed. Reading is on the rise.

To that end I hope that your reading of this book spurs you to develop your own library's core collection. I hope that you enjoy the work and even find a title or two that you had always meant to read. In this edition I include many additional websites and review sources, in print and online, that assist you in this process. Besides completely updating the bibliography in chapter 6, I also try to bring the reader up to date on what is happening in the development of e-books, digitization of books, and online mega-bookstores and their current impact on core selection. I have reexamined the sample core lists of the first edition, added a few selections as warranted, and am pleased to report that as promised the titles have aged extremely well. So, ultimately, do not let the headlines and continuing talk of the latest and greatest digital innovations deter you; remember that it is the content of a core title that is of the utmost importance, not how it is delivered.

Once again I would like to thank my husband and son for all their support and patience, and my personal readers, Sheila Levine, Susie Matazzoni, and Janice Russell, for their advice and help to a rusty librarian. Finally, I dedicate this revision to the memory of my dear friend and fellow bookworm, Jeanette Jenkins.

All that Mankind has done, thought, gained, or
been; it is lying as in magic preservation in the
pages of books. . . . All that a university or final
highest school can do for us is, still but what the
first school began doing—teach us to read.
—Thomas Carlyle, "The Hero as Man of Letters"

"OF MAKING OF MANY books, there is no end," according to Ecclesiastes 12:12. As librarian selectors, we certainly know this to be the delightful truth. Most librarians would be thrilled if libraries everywhere could afford to adopt the motto of London's amazing department store, Harrods: "Everything for Everybody, Everywhere." However, to our regret, we are too aware that we cannot include every newly published title in our collection, let alone retain all the titles we currently own. This is one of the most difficult aspects of librarianship: determining what titles to purchase and which pivotal works to make available on library shelves. It is also one of the most important, because librarianship is the only profession that dedicates itself to bringing books and information into the everyday lives of the world's citizens.

In the best-selling and much-discussed book by E. D. Hirsch Jr., *Cultural Literacy: What Every American Needs to Know*, the author lists items of basic information that range through the major fields of American life from sports to literature to science. Hirsch asserts that, in order to be effective in the modern world, a culturally literate person should know who Winnie the Pooh, Adolf Hitler, and Helen of Troy were; where the Highlands, the San Andreas Fault, and Puerto Rico are located; and what pasteurization, the Gallup poll, and the Library of Congress are. Hirsch argues for the "rediscovered insight that literacy is more than a skill based upon the knowledge that all of us unconsciously have about language. We know instinctively that to understand what somebody is saying, we must understand more than the surface meanings of words; we have to understand the context as well."[1]

This body of information—the geographic places, famous and infamous people, and historic events—can be found within the works that constitute a library's core collection. We come across this information daily, without clarification or explanation, in magazines, on the radio, on television, on the Internet, in the movies, in books and newspapers. It is assumed that we will understand, that we are informed—culturally literate. Hirsch concludes his book with a lengthy double-column list, "What Literate Americans Know," which is in essence a roll call of core titles, authors, and subjects that a library user should be able to locate in a public library regardless of its size.[2] Although written over two decades ago, *Cultural Literacy* still proves to be an excellent checklist of modern everyday knowledge, whether or not you agree with this type of list. This book is one of the many sources you can use to develop a list of core titles for libraries.

In his book *Faster: The Acceleration of Just about Everything*, James Gleick discusses the obsession in this country with time and efforts to stretch the 1,440 minutes that make up our day. He describes the acceleration of art and the ways we are programmed today to "jog more, read less." Our "grandparents might have read at least one newspaper in the morning and another in the evening. *USA Today* caters to your more modern reading habits by keeping its copy short. Other newspapers have catered to them by going out of business." Gleick cites one gloomy estimation showing that the average citizen spends "only sixteen minutes a day reading books and forty-one reading newspapers and magazines." If one accepts these figures, it quickly becomes obvious that only a fraction of a book can be read in a week. Gleick warns that, if you find yourself saying more and more often, "'I'm behind in my reading' . . . as though final term was ending and you had just discovered the mandatory reading list," this might be the moment to slow down and remember that, like other thoughtful activities, reading takes time.[3]

Why Read the Classics? a posthumously published compilation of essays by novelist Italo Calvino, agrees with Gleick's assessment of modern life's dearth of time for reading. Calvino asks the question, "Where can we find the time and the ease of mind to read the classics, inundated as we are by the flood of printed material about the present? . . . Reading the classics seems to be at odds with our pace of life, which does not tolerate long stretches of time" devoted to human-istic pursuits such as reading.[4] It behooves us to remember that Calvino's essay was written in 1981, before Gleick wrote his book and well before the Internet loomed over our lives, giving us access to incredible amounts of information at the stroke of a key. An article in *USA Today*, "Information Everywhere, but Not the Time to Think," outlines a study completed in 2000 at the University of California, Berkeley, that confirms what Calvino said almost thirty years ago: "We're awash in a sea of information, and the tide is rising." This comes as no surprise. What is most interesting about the results of the study, however, is that this information overload is largely generated by individuals. "Most information used to come from authoritative sources—governments, publishing houses, newspapers and magazines—and was edited before being made available to the public. . . . Now there are home videos, office documents, e-mail, and more.

With e-mail alone, we are creating 500 times as much information each year as the total of all Web pages."[5]

The Berkeley project group used the byte, the basic unit of measurement for digital information, to measure and compare the amount of information available today, whether it be text or electronic. A byte is the smallest discrete piece of binary information and is a unit of storage capable of holding a single character or letter or a space between words. The researchers estimated that the contents of the Library of Congress comprise 10 terabytes (a terabyte is a trillion bytes). Web pages at that time contained about 21 terabytes, and e-mail totaled some 11,285 terabytes. The professors who wrote this study concluded that soon "it will be possible for the average person to access virtually all recorded information."[6]

One cannot help but wonder what more than a decade of reading online and daily surfing on the Internet, overflowing with terabytes of information, has done to our ability to read in the conventional manner. Unlike browsing the Web, reading a book, whether it be an electronic or a printed book, requires a great deal of concentration and engagement. In the *Atlantic* article "Is Google Making Us Stupid?" author Nicholas Carr addresses this very concern: "Once I was a scuba diver in the sea of words. Now I zip along the surface like a guy on a Jet Ski." In a study of online research habits, Carr found that scholars from University College London discovered that we are currently in "the midst of a sea change in the way we read and think," and that people using online sites exhibit "a form of skimming activity," hopping from one source to another and rarely returning to any source they had already visited. They typically read no more than one or two pages of an article or book before they would "bounce" out to another site. These researchers maintain "that users are not reading online in the traditional sense; indeed there are signs that new forms of 'reading' are emerging as users 'power browse' horizontally through titles, contents pages and abstracts going for quick wins."[7]

In 2004 the National Endowment for the Arts reached a similar conclusion in its publication *Reading at Risk: A Survey of Literary Reading in America*. During this comprehensive survey of adults, researchers discovered that "the percentage of adult Americans reading literature has dropped dramatically over the past 20 years," and that "the decline in reading correlates with increased participation in a variety of electronic media, including the Internet."[8]

As librarians listening to these writers discuss the importance of cultural literacy coupled with the lack of time devoted to reading, and realizing the ever-increasing amount of information available to our clientele, we must be aware of the tremendous ramifications for libraries nationwide. Ultimately, these conditions create great uncertainty about how we are to approach librarianship in the years ahead. Certainly, these are exciting times to be information specialists, but as librarians we cannot help but question the future of the book and the role of libraries. The library is perhaps the last bastion against this information deluge, an orderly haven where classics wait to be discovered.

This is the role of a core collection, to ensure that these books and films are in stock when people come to find them, that libraries fulfill their promise to the next generation of readers.

THE IMPACT OF TECHNOLOGY

Over the past ten years the technology of the electronic book—or e-book, as it is most commonly called—has greatly matured, but the impact of this cyber-age book is still hard to predict. Nonetheless, it must be considered when writing about collection development. Anderson Consulting reported that by 2005 the sale of e-books would reach $2.3 billion. Other publishing polls at that time did not support this optimism. *Time Digital* predicted that the "e-book revolution will take hold slowly. The shift to e-books as a primary reading source will take at least 10 years." That neither of these predictions has proved to be correct is irrelevant. The important thing is that we are still in the midst of a "transformative moment in print culture. Breaking books down into a digital format—whether read with some sort of electronic device or as a traditional book via print-on-demand technology—is the key."[9]

The e-book continues to gain readers, and many libraries offer books that can be downloaded. The increasing popularity of the Kindle, Amazon's e-reader, has converted many additional users. Today these electronic book readers are still a novelty, though they certainly appear to be gaining disciples. The *New York Times* reports:

> Kindle buyers appear to be outside the usual gadget-hound demographic. Almost as many women as men are buying it . . . and the device is most popular among 55- to 64-year-olds. So far, publishers like Harper Collins, Random House and Simon & Schuster say that sales of e-books for any device—including simple laptop downloads—constitute less than 1 percent of total book sales. Publishers say sales of e-books have tripled or quadrupled in the last year.

Amazon has not been forthcoming about the number of Kindle readers it has sold since its launch two years ago, and estimates vary widely—from 260,000 units to a million.[10]

In the *Wall Street Journal* article "How the E-book Will Change the Way We Read and Write," author Steven Johnson posits that Amazon's Kindle has brought book reading to the brink of an absolute technological revolution:

> The book's migration to the digital realm would not be a simple matter of trading ink for pixels, but would likely change the way we read, write, and sell books in profound ways. It will make it easier for us to buy books, but at the same time make it easier to stop reading them. It will expand the universe of books at our fingertips. . . .

It will give writers and publishers the chance to sell more obscure books, but it may well end up undermining some of the core attributes that we have associated with book reading for more than 500 years. There is great promise and opportunity in the digital-books revolution. The question is: Will we recognize the book itself when the revolution has run its course?[11]

Whether Johnson's vision is accurate is still a matter of conjecture. At the 2009 Book Expo America, the book trade's annual show, publishers and authors acknowledged that there were, as editor Tina Brown said, "volcanic changes" confronting an "industry challenged on every side." Pulitzer Prize winner Richard Russo agreed that "we're all waiting for the next thing—whatever that is," but said he will keep writing "until they tell me I'm obsolete." Carol Fitzgerald of BookReporter.com worried that too much attention is going to "devices and formats and digitizing instead of books and authors."[12] National Book Award winner Sherman Alexie expressed his feeling that the expensive e-book readers were "elitist" and therefore he would not allow his novels to be made available in digital form.[13] Confusion continues to reign in the book industry, for no one truly knows what the eventual impact of the e-book will be and how it will ultimately affect our reading habits.

Perhaps *Time*'s Robert Boynton got it right over ten years ago when he wrote on the magazine's website that

> what Gutenberg's moveable type did for readers, the digitized book is doing for writers. . . . The entire publishing model is changing from print and distribute to distribute and then print. While publishers have traditionally overseen the form and content of books in the future they will concentrate on the content alone. "Precisely how you are going to read a book is irrelevant."[14]

The ever-popular Stephen King agrees that Kindle will not replace books but that it can be a useful tool for a reader; he was recruited to help launch Amazon's second-generation Kindle with a new "e-adventure," *UR*, which was available only for the new Kindle. In this novella, a college professor receives a pink alternate universe Kindle that allows him to read a Hemingway story that was never written and so allows King to muse on the future of the written word. King appears fascinated by his Kindle, as is his fictionalized Kindle owner, who lovingly describes many of the e-reader's features. In describing his first experiences with his new Kindle, King remarks that "for a while I was very aware that I was looking at a screen and bopping a button instead of turning pages. . . . Then the story simply swallowed me, as the good ones always do. It became about the message instead of the medium, and that's the way it's supposed to be."[15]

Stephen King makes an excellent point and one that we librarians can take heart from when we consider buying e-books for core collections. They are just another edition of a book with a different way of conveying words, but the content remains the same. And whether a core title is read on Kindle or in a tattered old edition, it is still the same book. Certainly e-books must be taken into account when determining how many copies of a title to buy for a library. Perhaps at some future date physically owning a printed copy of a title will no longer be necessary. Currently, however, we cannot predict how willing the average reader will be to use e-books or how widespread their use will ultimately become. After all, the book has a proven track record; it is portable and easy to use, and, most important, books are available for free to everyone with a library card. So whether the general public will embrace the e-book, only time will tell.

Over the course of the book's five-hundred-year history, every new technological advance, whether it be the radio, television, audiobooks, video games, or now e-books, has found doomsayers predicting the demise of the book. But it is the story and the information that are most important and that transcend technology. In the almost one hundred and fifty years since Charles Dickens died, not one of his twenty novels has ever gone out of print. His stories continue to find new readers—the quintessential core titles. Electronic books do not threaten libraries but enhance our collections, and people that invest in e-readers are first and foremost readers and therefore of primary importance to libraries. It is certainly possible to imagine entire libraries of e-books in the future, where readers "check out" titles by downloading them. But that still would not change the fundamental need for a core collection.

An interesting sidelight to this print revolution is that it will be a tremendous boon to the aspiring writer and will no doubt result in many more "books" being "self-published" electronically. For a small investment, would-be authors can issue their work for sale to the public online, entirely bypassing the traditional publishing industry. Such e-publishers as Xlibris and iUniverse are making it possible for "uncommercial" authors to be published and to determine their own markets. Writers submitting their manuscripts to a publishing website are assigned an ISBN to allow an eventual listing in *Books in Print* and receive a custom-designed cover, royalties, and free web promotion of their book along with a promise that their work will appear in major distribution databases for easy ordering. Technology has made it incredibly easy for just about anyone to publish a book quickly and inexpensively.

Harper's magazine was concerned about the potential volume of vanity titles that a "publishing services provider" such as Xlibris might provide. The article's authors estimated that in a few years

> Xlibris will be publishing 100,000 titles a year. That equals the 1999 output of all American publishers combined. . . . The publication of 100,000 mostly dubious books year after year will, in time, affect American publishing in every worst way and obliterate whatever remains of a genuine book culture. . . . The book publishing industry has many problems; publishing too few books is not one of them.[16]

Xlibris counters that, although it is uncertain whether "this explosion is 'good' or 'bad,' Xlibris was founded for the purpose of unleashing, to quote the *New York Times*, 'an outburst of self-expression unparalleled in our country's literary history.' We believe that everyone has a story to tell and that these stories should be preserved to add to the richness of humanity."[17] In 2008, Xlibris and its parent company Bertram Capital accounted for 19,000 titles, nearly six times more than Random House, the world's largest publisher of consumer books, released that year.[18] This is definitely a sizable number of books, but nowhere near the troublesome number *Harper's* predicted a decade ago. The amazing technology that results in ever-expanding bytes of information is humbling for today's librarian. Uncertainty faces librarians who must determine what course to follow when developing their general adult collections. This is even worse when they must create both fiction and all-subject core collections.

As we have seen, we are not alone in our bewilderment. James Surowiecki, writing for the *New Yorker* over a decade ago, expressed it eloquently when he said that "the advent of new technology has a way of turning all of us into either Trotskyites, preaching the inevitability and virtue of revolution, or reactionaries insisting that our Model T's are still just dandy. . . . The hardest thing to do is keep one foot in the old world while trying to step bravely into the new."[19] Despite the proliferation of digital technology in our libraries and its permeation of library literature, establishing a core collection that includes the classics and the best core books on pertinent subjects for the public's needs will become even more crucial as this information overload continues to overwhelm our library users. We are all aware of how intimidating our library collections can be with just our few measly terabytes. We see daily how our clientele gravitate to the book truck currently being shelved or to the new-book area, since these smaller groupings of books are so much less forbidding than the long range of book stacks that greet our users as they enter our buildings.

Librarians are still the most qualified to navigate the public through this onslaught of "bytes," whether they be print or electronic. As information specialists we understand where the information on the Internet comes from and that a high proportion of the Web's resources are strictly commercial sites. The Internet is certainly useful and extremely accessible, but its accuracy is a lot harder to judge. Google Search is a web search engine that indexes billions of web pages so that its users can research any subject they desire; its stated mission is to organize the world's information and make it universally accessible and useful. Today it is the most used search engine on the Web, with over 53 percent of the market share, well beyond Yahoo!'s 20 percent. But the thing to remember is that 99 percent of Google's revenue comes directly from advertising, as noted in its 2008 annual report. Yahoo!, the second most popular Internet directory, gathers its contents mostly from its users and proclaims in its service file disclaimer, "Yahoo! makes no representations concerning any endeavor to review the content of sites listed in the directory."[20] Much of the content of these websites would not stand up to even the lowest standards of many libraries' collection development policies and, if issued as a book, would not meet basic reference selection criteria of accuracy, impartiality, and accountability. There is no doubt that library users are increasingly in need of any assistance librarians can give them in finding the best sources of information, no matter in what format it might ultimately be delivered.

Ironically, writes Steven Johnson, "books are the dark matter of the information universe," for most of the millions of books published have

> largely been excluded from Google's index . . . because the modern infosphere is both organized and navigated through hyperlinked pages of digital text, with the most linked pages rising to the top of Google Inc.'s all-powerful search-results pages. This has led us toward some traditional forms of information, such as newspapers and magazines, as well as towards new forms, such as blogs and Wikipedia. But because books have largely been excluded from Google's index—distinct planets of unlinked analog text—that vast trove of knowledge can't complete with its hyperlinked rivals.[21]

In 2002, Google launched a "secret 'books' project." Google Book Search turned out to be an incredibly ambitious project to digitize the full text of the world's literature. By 2007, Google had digitized one million books; by 2008, seven million were added. Most of these scanned works are no longer in print or available commercially, and one million of them are no longer under copyright protection and are in the public domain. In 2006, Google began working with several major libraries to include their collections in the Google Books Library Project. Google's ultimate goal as stated on its website is "to create a comprehensive, searchable, virtual card catalog of all books in all languages. . . . If the book is out of copyright, you'll be able to view and download the entire book."

With the advent of Kindle and the Google Books Library Project, millions of digitized books will become available to be searched electronically for the first time. The future ramifications of this project along with the other technological developments that have been discussed here are impossible to predict. But even in the midst of this incredible electronic revolution, I maintain that most librarians can still agree with Helen Haines's assessment in her classic, *Living with Books: The Art of Book Selection*, of the importance and glory of books and reading:

> Books give a deeper meaning and interest to living. There is nothing in daily work, in the most humdrum occupation, that cannot be made more interesting or more useful through books. They are means to proficiency in every calling. They are inexhaustible sources of pleasure. They bring to us the life of the world as it was and as it is now. They supply increased resources. Those able to

turn to books for companionship are seldom lonely; nor do they suffer from the need of finding some action, however trivial, to fill an empty hour. They have friends who will come when desired, bringing amusement, counsel. . . . Books impart deepened sensitiveness to ideals, to beauty, to pleasure, to the best emotions of life. . . . To recognize these overtones, to catch their delicate implications and glimpse their variant elusive radiations, is one of the keenest and most enduring pleasures of life. This is the "meaning of culture."[22]

Technology aside for the moment, the difficulty for us as librarians is determining which of the myriad books published actually accomplishes what Haines so eloquently describes. How do busy librarians find these cornerstones of culture and, furthermore, how do we make certain that our library stocks and retains these classic titles? This is ultimately the crux of core collection development.

CLASSICS AS CORE TITLES

In July 1998, the editorial board of the Modern Library, a division of the Random House Publishing Trade Group founded in 1917 to provide the world's best literature at a reasonable cost, issued its list of the hundred best twentieth-century novels in the English language. This list was published in the *New York Times* and immediately generated an astonishing amount of discussion. Random House's website reported that more than 400,000 avid readers went online to cast votes for their favorite books. Shortly after, a follow-up article appeared in *Newsweek*. It soon became apparent that people truly cared about what books were on this list and were equally concerned about books that were excluded. *Newsweek* felt it was so important that it published the entire list. "You keep hearing that we live in a post-literate age," the magazine marveled, but "how do you explain what went on last week? . . . a surprising number of people were obsessing over a list of the century's 100 greatest English-language novels, from James Joyce's 'Ulysses' (no. 1) to Booth Tarkington's 'The Magnificent Ambersons' (no. 100)." *Newsweek* was not surprised that only six of the hundred were from the past quarter-century with only one—William Kennedy's *Ironweed*—from the past fifteen years, since the Modern Library board of "distinguished white poohbahs" had an average age of sixty-nine.[23] The *Los Angeles Times* noted that fifty-nine of the titles were published by Random House or one of its many divisions. The newspaper also questioned why only eight women were included on the list, none of them black, and why only one author, Salman Rushdie, was born later than 1932.[24] *Library Journal* surveyed its readers and quickly responded with a list of its own, as did students of the Radcliffe College publishing course. Koen Book Distributors queried its bookseller clientele for their one hundred favorite novels of the twentieth century. All this hubbub did not faze Modern Library's board chair, Christopher Cerf. On the contrary, Cerf claimed that he "was delighted with all the carping and nit-picking. 'It's a neat game,' he said. 'Here we are talking about it, and it's going in *Newsweek*, so it's working.'"[25] Random House staff members maintained all along that their purpose was to get people talking about great books, and, according to the Random House website, they felt that they "succeeded beyond [their] wildest imaginings."

Discussions about what are the best and most important books are familiar to librarians. Over the years there have been ongoing debates in library circles about this topic and about the more immediate question of whether a library should even buy or attempt to keep these "classics." Charlie Robinson, former director of the Baltimore County Public Library, was the most visible advocate with his "give 'em what they want" style of collection development—meaning lots of best-sellers. Robinson and his deputy director, Jean-Barry Molz, came to Baltimore from two of the more traditional libraries in the country, the Free Library of Philadelphia and Enoch Pratt Library, respectively, and they are the first to admit that they were both

> raised in the tradition of the great collections—making sure you gave people the definitive works of literature. When we came the intent was to make Baltimore County a "good" library. We soon saw that it was ridiculous. It was insane. . . . We bought many books that as librarians we felt it was necessary to have. And they didn't move. . . . What was the point of giving them what they didn't want?[26]

Arguments continue about whether the classics are still read and whether they have any validity in today's society. Perhaps the one place that the classics are still read regularly is in our colleges, where they are discussed, dissected, and analyzed in obligatory term papers, but often there is little joy in their reading. So it is not surprising that librarians themselves often have a predisposition to assume that the classics are dull and that no one chooses to read them anymore. Therefore, this reasoning continues, there is no need to stock the classics, except perhaps in a central library, which many believe has tons of room and too much money anyway.

Changing Lives Through Literature (CLTL) also requires reading classics, but this "must-read" program is mandated by a judge. An alternative to incarceration, CLTL uses selected classics to reach criminal offenders. The program began in 1991 when eight men—with over 148 convictions between them, many of whom never graduated high school—were sentenced to probation instead of prison if they completed a twelve-week modern American literature course with Professor Waxler at the University of Massachusetts Dartmouth. This program and similar applications have since expanded throughout the United States and England. In 2003 it was awarded an Exemplary Education grant from the National Endowment for the Humanities. CLTL is founded on the premise that reading and discussing the great works of classic writers such as Jack London, James Baldwin, and John Steinbeck, criminal offenders can "begin to investigate and explore aspects of themselves. . . . Instead of seeing their world from one angle, they began opening up to new perspectives and started realizing that they had choices in life. Thus, literature became a road to insight."[27] In her recent essay "Read a Book, Get out of Jail," Harvard professor Leah Price analyses the CLTL program and notes that it is much like probation rulings that require attending twelve-step programs:

> There's nothing surprising about the idea that certain books teach lessons. . . . Here, though, the medium becomes the message: the art of reading changes—or as we used to say, converts—the reader, even when the texts being read contain no explicit moral injunctions. Like Sunday school pupils, graduates of Changing Lives Through Literature are given a book along with their diploma. It hardly matters that the traditional leatherette Bible is replaced by a sleek black volume from the Library of America.[28]

The dispute concerning the necessity of stocking classics in today's libraries is only a prelude to heated discussions about what constitutes a classic. What is a core title? Although many agree that libraries should stock the classics and core titles, people have varying ideas on what criteria define core books. This argument always reminds me of the split-screen scene in Woody Allen's *Annie Hall* in which both Allen and Diane Keaton are visiting their respective therapists, who ask them "How often do you have sex?" Keaton replies, "All the time, at least three times a week," and Allen says, "Hardly at all, just three times a week." Similarly with core books, seemingly objective criteria can become subjective. In the hopes of avoiding this Annie Hall kind of perceptual confusion, I include specific titles throughout this book to illustrate the different principles of core collections being discussed. Sample subject core lists in the final chapter can be starting points for developing your library's own core collection, for use in training, or as a jumping-off point for further in-house discussion.

Columbia University professor Andrew Delbanco, in his book *Required Reading: Why Our American Classics Matter Now*, demonstrates the importance of certain classic writers, such as Edith Wharton, Herman Melville, Henry Thoreau, and Richard Wright, and how they have all added to our common heritage and continue to remain indispensable to our culture. Professor Delbanco further expresses his gratitude to these great thinkers and celebrates "them because I have no doubt that the world is better for their having written, and because I believe it is the responsibility of the critic to incite others to read them."[29]

Mortimer Adler, editor of the *Encyclopaedia Britannica*, is the man most closely associated with the entire Great Books approach to continuing education.

In 1946, as associate editor of the fifty-four-volume *Great Books of the Western World*, he advocated that the public get together and regularly discuss a classic. He maintained that "the fundamental ideas and concepts upon which education should be based are not merely the mores and beliefs which happen to be current in twentieth-century America. . . . They are universal truths about what constitutes a good education for all men at all times and places." Adler wanted everyone to read the Great Books and maintained that they could be understood by anyone with the "gumption" to read them and that learning never stops: "Our minds, unlike our bodies, are able to grow and develop until death overtakes us."[30] In the late 1960s, the concept of Great Books, with its sole emphasis on the writing of "dead white males," was questioned and fell out of favor. Today, however, Great Books reading groups are gaining popularity, and once again discussion groups are meeting regularly in libraries.

A Great Idea at the Time: The Rise, Fall, and Curious Afterlife of the Great Books, written by *Boston Globe* columnist Alex Beam, is a surprisingly witty look at how Encyclopaedia Britannica and the University of Chicago launched the *Great Books of the Western World*, "with a set of deluxe, faux-leather Great Books, all fifty-four volumes of them . . . purporting to encompass all of Western knowledge from Homer to Freud."[31] What is most interesting for our purposes about Beam's history are his thoughts on the Great Books' legacy today. How different is Oprah's Book Club, which in 2004 helped sell over a million copies of Tolstoy's classic *Anna Karenina*? Or the constant ads in the *New York Times* and *Wall Street Journal* touting the Teaching Company with its Great Courses DVDs? Or the Roberto Clemente Family Guidance Center in Manhattan, which started teaching the Great Books in 1997 in the belief that "the best education for the best is the best education for all"? Beam concludes that "the Great Books are dead. Long live the Great Books!"[32]

I agree with Delbanco's, Adler's, and Beam's assessments that beautiful writing lasts, well-defined characters last, and compelling narrative lasts. Writing survives long after ideas go extinct—particularly if the writing is exceptionally good. Today there can be no more important function for any library than to supply these important works to its citizens. The premise of *Developing an Outstanding Core Collection* is that certain basic titles are the foundation of any library. These core titles include the essential classics—Great Books, if you will—that are read by generation after generation as well as seminal works that reflect and shed light on the events of humankind. They are the books that define history and are hallmarks of the written word.

CORE TITLES AND COLLECTION DEVELOPMENT

Core titles interpret a subject in an eye-opening way that allows us to visit worlds we have never experienced or to explain a previously incomprehensible subject in a manner that many can understand. Rachel Carson's *Silent Spring* and James Watson's book on the discovery of DNA, *The Double Helix*, are two such books. Core books change the way we think, the way we comprehend a subject we never thought about before. They all share the power of the written word. Some are books that altered the course of history, like Marx's *Communist Manifesto* and *Quotations from Chairman Mao Zedong*. Others have imparted knowledge that illuminates our lives—for example, Sigmund Freud's *Interpretation of Dreams*, Dr. Benjamin Spock's *Common Sense Book of Baby and Child Care*, and Alex Comfort's *Joy of Sex*. There are books that make us rethink the way we view the world and the events that shaped it, such as *The Autobiography of Malcolm X*, Anne Frank's *Diary of a Young Girl*, and John Hersey's *Hiroshima*. Core books like Randy Shilts's *And the Band Played On*, essential reading on the AIDS epidemic, Upton Sinclair's *The Jungle*, on the meatpacking industry, and Jessica Mitford's *American Way of Death*, on the funeral business, have fueled political debate and changed our nation's laws.

Core titles are the foundation of what makes a library a library; they provide the consistency that people expect to find in their libraries as they move from one stage of life to the next or from one community to another. Edwin S. Holmgren, director of the branch libraries of the New York Public Library, and William D. Walker, director of the research libraries, expressed this philosophy quite vividly in the introduction to their library's book list, "Books of the Century," which was issued to commemorate the library's first century: "For the librarians of the New York Public Library, books and the word are our passionate concern, and getting both to readers is our great enterprise."[33]

Core titles are the books people assume they will find at their library. Although our clients are always pleased to discover that we have Internet access, tax forms, concerts, or a guest author, they ultimately expect their library to provide books. Library patrons may express pleasure over a lecture series or at being able to register to vote at their local library; nonetheless, they expect to find a copy of *The Scarlet Letter* and would be dismayed to learn that their library no longer stocks this classic. Stocking core titles is one very sure way of giving your library users exactly what they want and hope to find at their library.

Surprisingly, the public's assumption that libraries will always have the classics along with the best books available on any given subject is not something all librarians would agree is the purpose of a library. The general public and our elected officials are mostly unaware that this is an area of debate in libraries and that there is limited consistency in the acquisition of basic works within library systems, much less within the same branch. Furthermore, library administrators may give short shrift to developing their library's collections. Although they might give lip service to the importance of collection development, they grant librarians minimal off-desk time to work on collections and provide limited selection training for staff members. Many administrators, and librarians themselves, believe that librarians instinctively know what books to buy and which to retain. How librarians are to obtain this knowledge is never explained. It is assumed that all librarians love books, read lots of them, and, therefore, will always know what to select, what to weed, and what to keep in their collections. Unfortunately, this is not the case. Sadly, librarians may even get defensive if they are called upon to account for what they have purchased.

Most librarians take only a single collection development class in library school. In this class, instructors are expected to teach the rudiments of selection and collection development, the issues of intellectual freedom and censorship, needs assessment, collection statements, deselection, budgets, vendors, gifts, and more. They are supposed to complete this course of study in just one semester, in addition to addressing the different types of libraries, whether they be academic, school, or public, no matter their size or budget.

Some librarians attend local or national library conferences where aisle after aisle of circulation systems, security systems, and technology products greet them. They see far fewer publishers' booths, and those that exhibit often showcase only limited books, most of them reference titles or children's books. Over the past decade, librarians have begun to realize that if they want to see books they need to attend the yearly trade show BookExpo America (BEA), formerly known as the American Booksellers Association Convention and Trade Exhibit. The American Booksellers Association (ABA) was founded in 1900 as a trade organization devoted to meeting the needs of independently owned bookstores with store front locations through advocacy, education, research, and information dissemination. The ABA supports free speech, literacy, and programs that encourage children to read. BEA, put on by the ABA, is North America's premier book event, designed to meet the needs of the entire book industry. Over 1,500 companies showcase their books, with many of the major U.S. publishers present, along with small and medium-sized presses and international publishers.

Years ago, librarians attending BEA were not given a warm reception by many of the publisher exhibitors and were actually snubbed by others. Publishers did not seem to understand that librarians had book budgets and actually bought books, often in larger quantities than many bookstores. After much advocacy on the part of ALA and its members, and the support of the major publishers' library marketing representatives, librarians are now accepted and welcomed at the show. With the decline of the independent bookseller, the growth of nationwide chain stores and warehouses, and the increase in librarian participation, it is conceivable that soon more librarians than booksellers will attend this yearly publishing event.

A search of library literature reveals surprisingly little on the actual day-to-day mechanics of adult collection development and the specific techniques used to select books. Yet throughout this literature it is apparent that librarians and their clientele care deeply about the written word and feel that books, even in this age of the emerging e-books, still are of primary importance to libraries. Apparently Microsoft cofounder Paul Allen agrees. The Associated Press reported that his foundation donated $20 million to the very fortunate Seattle Public Library, of which $15 million was earmarked to buy new books.[34]

Our federal government also made a commitment to literature and reading when it launched its Big Read program in 2006 to "bring the transformative power of literature into the lives of Americans . . . by providing citizens with the opportunity to read and discuss a single work within their communities."[35] A direct response to the disturbing decline reported in the National Endowment for the Arts report *Reading at Risk*, the Big Read attempts to organize, publicize, and finance programs to encourage people across their states to read selected Big Read books together.

Most of what has been written on selection is geared to children's books, reference materials, censorship, and written collection policy statements or is so general as to be of little help to the practicing librarian. The goal of this book is to supply answers to the following crucial questions: Where are librarians to get the necessary expertise to create and maintain their collections? How are they to develop collections that reflect their communities, have validity for their patrons, and contain the fundamental works of our society?

ONE LIBRARY'S JOURNEY

During my tenure as collection development coordinator for the Phoenix Public Library, our staff began a project to develop core collections in the system's ten branches and the Central Library. We already utilized core collections for periodicals and one for reference materials. Both of these were tiered collections, allowing for flexibility among agencies depending on size, budget, and use. Periodical core collections required some magazines to be purchased by every library agency. Detailed mandates defined which titles were to be retained and for how long. Reference books were included on their own core list on the basis of selection standards of accuracy, currency, ease of use, arrangement, authority, and, of course, expense. Grant monies were allocated to bring all the branches up to these core standards, and standing orders were established, when available, for each reference title. A yearly review of both the periodical and reference core lists allowed input from all librarians.

Developing and implementing these two core collections went smoothly. Most of the librarians appeared quite pleased to have these chores done for them centrally while retaining their ability to have a say in creating these essential collections. With the advent of the reference core collection, the Phoenix Public Library no longer had out-of-date reference books—no encyclopedia was ever more than four years old and no reference travel book over two years old. All branches and the Central Library received these core reference titles automatically as soon as they were published. It was a perfect world.

Naively, some librarians felt that creating core adult circulating collections was a logical outgrowth of our very successful reference and periodical core collections, and that the idea would be welcomed by librarians systemwide. This was not the case at all. Problems arose almost immediately. Staff were uncomfortable with even the most basic definition of what constituted a core title. Concerns emerged about the choice of staff responsible for the ultimate decision to designate a title as core. Questions arose about whose budget should pay for these "extra" books that all librarians were required to purchase, even though they might not want them or feel there was any need for them in their agencies. Branches with lower budgets complained they had not one extra dollar to spend on these required titles. Smaller agencies said they had no room for core titles that would not circulate and just take up much-needed shelf space. Librarians at the Central Library saw no reason to buy a particular core title when they had plenty of other books on the subject already. The only point of agreement among all agencies, no matter their size, was that the librarian selectors had enough to do already with providing weekly selection lists and serving on yearly add and replacement committees without adding core list creation.

It soon became apparent that there existed absolutely no staff buy-in to this core project. *Core* became the new four-letter word at the Phoenix Public Library. Even to this day, over twenty years later, if you were to ask the librarians who were around during this tumultuous process about the creation of the core collection, you would most likely receive quite an earful. As you might imagine, most of it is not flattering.

By 1986, however, the city librarian and the administration were convinced that core collections were much needed for the users of the Phoenix Public Library. The library system held relatively new collections. We were regularly adding new branches, and the Central Library was beginning to become a true central library, with tremendous breadth and depth to its collection; up to this point, the Central Library had essentially been not much more than the largest branch library. The administration suspected that the Central Library was located smack in the middle of one of the fastest-growing cities in the country, and their assumption proved correct. The U.S. Census Bureau's 1999 estimates revealed that when "compared with other parts of the country, growth in Phoenix and its suburbs made our Valley the fastest-growing among the nation's twenty largest metropolitan areas over the past decade."[36]

The city of Phoenix had no tradition of a great public library, and the library had no established collections that had been cultivated over the years. Many of the citizens of Phoenix were transplants from eastern and midwestern cities with some of this nation's most extraordinary public libraries. These new residents expected and demanded of their adopted city's library the same excellence they had in their original hometown libraries. Many of them wanted and anticipated that they would receive the same services and access to the same strong, highly developed collections to which they were accustomed in their hometowns. The administration insisted that work on this circulating core collection begin immediately with the new fiscal buying cycle. In retrospect, it was a good decision, for otherwise this project might never have begun. The incredible population growth of the city made it almost mandatory that the library's collection be immediately expanded and enriched. Waiting would have meant that the library would never catch up with the city's amazing growth.

Although immediate implementation ensured that the core collection plan would become a reality, additional preparation would have helped the librarians know exactly what was required of them and would have made them more comfortable with the work they were asked to accomplish. At the very least, the writing of a rudimentary selection statement for staff use would have gone a long way in helping selectors achieve the goal of creating a systemwide core collection.[37]

Looking back, it is surprising that no one thought about writing such a simple selection policy, for it was already required that all selectors in the Central Library write a policy for each of their assigned subject selection areas. These policies were reviewed and revised on a three-year cycle. The lack of a basic written collection development policy statement created much angst and confusion for the entire librarian staff, for the "Annie Hall" conundrum was never addressed. To help your library avoid this omission, chapter 2 suggests ways to write different types of collection development policy statements for core collections. It includes an outline and a sample core collection development policy statement that can serve as a model as librarians begin to work on creating the library's core collection.

How did the Phoenix Public Library manage to go from this chaotic beginning to ultimately create a systemwide adult circulating core collection that was universally accepted by its librarians? How did the core collection become a source of pride for them and the core meetings and forums some of their favorite work gatherings (the only ones where you actually talked about books!)? It was not an easy process, but it turned out to be an extremely worthwhile one.

As it turned out, most of the much-maligned core titles did circulate and, in some cases, even ended up increasing branch circulation. The core lists became quite attractive to other libraries throughout Arizona. Staff members were asked to speak on this topic at state conferences. Sample lists were often requested and sent to libraries around the country as well as to Australia, New Zealand, Canada, and England. The complete set of core lists, which covered the entire Dewey range, was purchased by several of these libraries, including the Library of Congress. Monies from the sale of the core lists went into a library education fund to help send staff members to training workshops and conferences, since clearly it was through their valiant efforts that these lists were developed. Throughout this guidebook, I explain the procedures that the Phoenix Public Library used and interject the lessons we learned—often the hard way—in the hope that your library's core collection creation will go far more smoothly than ours did.

CORE TITLES DEFINED

To this point I have used the term *core title* casually and assumed a certain understanding on the part of the reader. But exactly what is a core title? Many would answer, "It's a classic." Others would reply that core titles are those books we had to read in school, the ones that hardly ever circulate today. Let me begin by saying that one of the basic tenets of core collection development is that all core titles must circulate, not necessarily like Oprah selections or the latest best-seller, but they must be of current interest to library users. So although all core titles are great books, not all Great Books are core titles. Core collections, like the rest of the general collection, must also reflect the community's uniqueness, so there is always some variance among individual libraries' core collections. The Phoenix Public Library required that a core title circulate a minimum of three times within a given year in each and every agency to be retained as a designated core title. Core titles that fulfilled this basic requirement had to be stocked in all branch and Central Library collections. No library—with the possible exception of some very large central libraries or university libraries—has enough shelf space to waste on books that never circulate. Aware that we would be requiring every branch and the Central Library to purchase these core titles, no matter their size or budget, we agreed to use the most stringent of criteria when designating any title as core. Therefore, our number-one guiding principle of core selection was "When in doubt, just leave it out."

According to the *Random House Dictionary of the English Language*, a *classic* is "of the first or highest quality, class, or rank." Other definitions are "of literary or historical renown"; "an author or a literary work of the first rank, esp. one of demonstrably enduring quality"; "a work that is honored as definitive in its field."

Calvino, in his collection of essays on the classics, has a marvelous list of what he terms "definitions" of a classic, which can be used to answer the question he poses in his title, *Why Read the Classics?* His criteria include the following:

> The classics are those books about which you usually hear people saying: "I'm rereading . . . ," never "I'm reading . . ."

> The classics are those books which constitute a treasured experience for those who have read and loved them; but they remain just as rich an experience for those who reserve the chance to read them for when they are in the best condition to enjoy them.

> The classics are books which exercise a particular influence, both when they imprint themselves on our imagination as unforget-table, and when they hide in the layers of memory disguised as the individual's or the collective unconscious.

> A classic is a book which with each reading offers as much of a sense of discovery as the first reading.

> A classic is a book which has never exhausted all it has to say to its readers.

> The classics are those books which come to us bearing the aura of previous interpretations, and trailing behind them the traces

they have left in the culture or cultures (or just in the languages and customs) through which they have passed.

A classic is a work which constantly generates a pulviscular cloud of critical discourse around it, but which always shakes the particles off.

A classic is the term given to any book which comes to represent the whole universe, a book on a par with ancient talismans.[38]

The *Random House Dictionary* defines *core* more loosely: "the central, innermost, or most essential part of anything." If this is so, are core titles classics? Certainly a core fiction title often is a classic, and there would most likely be agreement among librarians that *The Scarlet Letter* is a classic, does circulate, and should be included in any core collection. Hawthorne's book, on occasion, still makes the *USA Today* best-seller list, particularly toward the end of August as students rush to do their summer reading before school resumes. Most of us would also agree that *Pride and Prejudice*—Jane Austen being one of the favorite authors of librarians—should be included in any core fiction list. But should all her work be included if Austen is considered a classic writer? Should all of Thomas Hardy, including *The Mayor of Casterbridge* and *Under the Greenwood Tree*? All of Dickens? Certainly *David Copperfield*, but what about *Nicholas Nickleby* or *The Mystery of Edwin Drood*? These books all meet the dictionary's definition of *classic*.

Once you venture beyond these classics into modern literature, the lines become even muddier. For example, are *Gone with the Wind* and *Ben Hur* classics? Should they be included on a fiction core list? Dare I even ask about Stephen King? Are his works classics? Is everything he wrote a modern classic, or is just *Carrie*? What about *The Stand*, considered by many to be his best book? Should every title written by a classic author be considered a core title? Should every ALA award–winning book be included? Every National Book Award winner? Every Pulitzer Prize winner? Every Big Read selection? Every book on Mortimer Adler's Great Books list? Enough!

You can see without a doubt that creating a core collection is a difficult task. These few examples clearly demonstrate how essential it is that there be staff discussion followed by the writing of criteria before any library attempts to develop a core collection. Anything from a completely separate core collection development policy statement to a brief addendum to a library's formal collection development policy statement will assist core selectors and help ensure consistency when they begin working together to develop a core collection.

OBJECTIVES AND PREMISE

Developing an Outstanding Core Collection is intended to train working librarians and library students in the methods for deciding which books to choose as core titles. This guide acknowledges that library collections are often designed for different purposes and diverse communities and assumes that most libraries already have some type of written collection policy statement to which a core component can be added. If not, I hope that at the very least your library has put some thought into creating a library-specific management program that organizes this complex process of selection. Most important, I assume that you, the reader, agree that a classic body of literature of great value to libraries and society exists today.

This book is designed to give librarians a practical guide, so the emphasis is on those aspects of collection development that are necessary for the creation of adult core collections; I offer limited discussion of selection components that pertain only to general collections. The bibliography in chapter 6 lists titles that address general collection development topics and that provide logical and universal assistance in developing core collections.

Developing an Outstanding Core Collection offers detailed instructions on how to determine what constitutes a core title, how to gather information on these titles, and how to maintain an up-to-date, viable, and utilized core collection. It provides instructions on limiting the subjectivity of judgment about the importance of a title and getting staff and knowledgeable members of the community involved in the process. It assumes that every librarian on staff has expertise in some subject area, is well read in some fiction genre, or knows a specific author's works well and, therefore, should be involved in the core list development project. Creation of a core collection must tap into the book knowledge of the "experts" on staff. This guide also presumes that staff members are interested in literature and in the quality of their collections and are committed to developing a core collection for their library.

A carefully thought-out core collection enables the library user to find top-notch titles in most subjects, thereby relieving selectors of the burden of worrying that the library does not have high-quality books on major subjects of interest. Selectors are assured that the library has the most important works on any given subject and representative books for the community. Furthermore, a core title list can assist in addressing citizen complaints, for library staff can use it to show members of the public which titles on a given subject are required systemwide purchases. I have found this to be particularly helpful as a public relations tool with community groups that may be anxious about the overall quality of the collection or about a single subject area within the library. For example, when dealing with the concerns of religious or cultural organizations, staff can demonstrate that the library has purchased the basic books in their area of interest through a core title list, and that these titles are available to be checked out at every library agency. Librarians can show concerned citizens a precise list of titles that have been purchased on a subject and tell them who in the community assisted in selecting these core titles or which standard bibliographic sources were consulted. When presented with all the thought and work that have gone into purchasing these basic books for the library, special interest groups generally are reassured that their subject needs have been considered carefully and met by the library staff. Of course, this assumes that core list creation has been done well and can stand up to this type of intense scrutiny.

Creating a viable core collection that reflects your community, does not bankrupt your book budget, and is well utilized is not an easy task. It takes commitment and determination on the part of both the library staff and its administration. The foundational principle of core collection development is that books and literature matter and need to be preserved. National Book Award winner Susan Sontag went even farther: "Matters is surely too pale a word [to use for literature]. That there are books that are 'necessary,' that is, books that while reading them, you know you'll reread. Maybe more than once. Is there a greater privilege than to have a consciousness expanded by, filled with, pointed to literature?"[39]

Our collections are what make us unique and what grant us our place in society. There are other agencies that have teen centers or supply tax forms and bus passes, but only the library—most particularly the public library—purchases books for the general public to meet their recreational and educational needs. The public library with its reservoir of titles enables books to be a part of everyone's daily life, no matter the level of income or education. The public library is truly, as Thomas Carlyle implied in this chapter's epigraph, the people's university, and core collections are crucial to fulfilling this function.

Notes

1. E. D. Hirsch Jr., *Cultural Literacy: What Every American Needs to Know* (Boston: Houghton Mifflin, 1987), 3.
2. Ibid., 152–215.
3. James Gleick, *Faster: The Acceleration of Just about Everything* (New York: Pantheon, 1999), 130.
4. Italo Calvino, *Why Read the Classics?* trans. Martin McLaughlin (New York: Pantheon, 1999), 7–8.
5. Elizabeth Weise, "Information Everywhere, but Not the Time to Think," *USA Today*, October 19, 2000, D1.
6. Ibid., D10.
7. Nicholas Carr, "Is Google Making Us Stupid?" *Atlantic Online*, July/August 2008, 1, 2.
8. *Reading at Risk: A Survey of Literary Reading in America* (Washington, D.C.: National Endowment for the Arts, 2004).
9. Robert S. Boynton, "You Say You Want an E-book Revolution?" Time Digital, December 2000, 40.
10. Brad Stone and Motoko Rich, "Turning Page, E-books Start to Take Hold," *New York Times*, December 24, 2008, A1, A16.
11. Steven Johnson, "How the E-book Will Change the Way We Read and Write," *Wall Street Journal*, April 20, 2009, R1–3.
12. Bob Minzesheimerm, "Power of Digital Looms over Expo," *USA Today*, June 1, 2009, D5.
13. Motoko Rich, "Book Fair Buzz Is Not Contained between 2 Covers," *New York Times*, June 1, 2009, C1.

14. Boynton, "You Say You Want," 42–46.
15. Jerry Harkavy, "King Book Kindles Big Interest with E-readers," *Arizona Republic*, March 8, 2009, E9.
16. Tom Bissell and Webster Younce, "All Is Vanity," *Harper's*, December 2000, 58–59.
17. Roland LaPlante, "Perish or Publish," *Harper's*, March 2001, 4.
18. Motoko Rich, "Bright Passage in Publishing: Authors Who Pay Their Way," *New York Times*, January 29, 2009, A19.
19. James Surowiecki, "Books Will Endure, but Will Publishers?" *New Yorker*, June 19 and 26, 2000, 75.
20. Laura B. Cohen, "Yahoo! and the Abdication of Judgment," *American Libraries*, January 2001, 60–61.
21. Johnson, "How the E-book," R3.
22. Helen E. Haines, *Living with Books: The Art of Book Selection*, 2nd ed. (New York: Columbia University Press, 1950), 5–6.
23. David Gates and Ray Sawhill, "The Dated and the Dead," *Newsweek*, August 3, 1998, 64.
24. Wanda Coleman, "Checking the List Twice," *Los Angeles Times* (home edition), July 22, 1998.
25. Gates and Sawhill, "Dated and the Dead," 64.
26. Nancy Pearl, "Gave 'Em What They Wanted," *Library Journal*, September 1, 1996, 136.
27. Changing Lives Through Literature, "History." http://cltl.umassd.edu.
28. Leah Price, "Read a Book, Get out of Jail," *New York Times Book Review*, March 1, 2009.
29. Andrew Delbanco, *Required Reading: Why Our American Classics Matter Now* (New York: Farrar, Straus and Giroux, 1997), 214.
30. Adler quote in Richard Nilsen, "M. Adler Dies at 98; Influential Educator," *Arizona Republic*, June 30, 2001, A17.
31. Alex Beam, *A Great Idea at the Time: The Rise, Fall, and Curious Afterlife of the Great Books* (New York: PublicAffairs, 2008), 1.
32. Ibid., 196–201.
33. "Books of the Century" (New York: New York Public Library, 1995); later published as Elizabeth Diefendorf, ed., *New York Public Library's Books of the Century* (New York: Oxford University Press, 1996).
34. The remaining $5 million was given to help build a children's center for the new central library. "Seattle PL Gets $20-Million Gift," *American Libraries*, October 2000, 21.
35. "The Big Read" (Washington, D.C.: National Endowment for the Arts, 2006).
36. According to Hernan Rozemberg, "Phoenix Growth Tops Major Cities," *Arizona Republic*, October 20, 2000, A1.
37. For the purposes of this book, I use the term *selector* to designate a person responsible for making the core selection decisions as well as developing and managing the library's core collection. This term acknowledges that in some libraries the staff members performing selection and collection development duties may not be librarians. Additional job titles that can be used interchangeably with *selector* include *bibliographic specialist, collection manager* or *developer,* and *subject specialist.*
38. Calvino, *Why Read the Classics?* 3–7.
39. Susan Sontag, "Directions: Write, Read, Rewrite. Repeat Steps 2 and 3 as Needed," *New York Times*, December 18, 2000, B1–2.

CHAPTER 2

DEVELOPING A CORE COLLECTION POLICY STATEMENT

*Books are the treasured wealth of the world and
the fit inheritance of generations and nations.*
—Henry David Thoreau, *Walden*

SELECTING BOOKS FOR A core collection is probably the most satisfying collection development task a librarian can perform. Creating a core collection is a pure and unadulterated celebration of books and the joys of reading. Most librarians will tell you that this love of books and reading is the number-one reason they went into the profession. Librarians often admit that they are addicted to books and bookstores and that they have far too many books with not nearly enough space or shelves in their homes for all of them. Brenda Knight, in her charming book *Women Who Love Books Too Much*, describes the telling symptoms of this special breed of book lover to which most librarians, whatever their gender, would claim a kinship: "Does your heart race when you see a new book by one of your favorite authors? Do you feel a little dizzy when you walk into a bookstore packed with hundreds of new books? . . . Do you read the book review section of the newspaper before your horoscope?"[1] If you have answered yes to these questions, either you are a man or woman who loves books too much or, more likely, you are a librarian. Librarians would be the first to empathize with the book lover's plight described in this *Los Angeles Times* news brief "Man Almost Killed by Books":

> Friends and neighbors said Anthony P. Cima, the 87-year-old San Diego man who was buried under thousands of books in Sunday's earthquake, had recently counted the volumes in his room and by his tally, there were 9,900 hardcover copies in his 12-foot-square hotel-apartment. . . . Fire Department spokesman Larry Stewart said it took firefighters about 20 minutes just to locate Cima's foot and another 20 minutes to get him out.[2]

Selecting titles for a core collection assumes that the selector has, in addition to a love of books, an extensive knowledge of literature or subject expertise along with the professional skills to evaluate the merits of any given title. This assumption is the conundrum of core title selection and the reason I wrote this book—to assist librarians in becoming savvy core selectors by providing specific steps and examples. When purchasing for a core collection, the librarian decides what to buy on the basis of literary merit and the value of a title. Core selectors are looking to buy the best book on a subject, unencumbered by the often-debilitating restrictions of public demand or best-sellerdom that today dictate so much of the selection work done for public libraries. When buying core titles, selectors are often purchasing titles they have read and personally enjoyed, books they are eager to share with the reading portion of their community who love books as much as they do—the Anthony Cimas, if you will. Tell a well-read librarian about a book you particularly enjoyed and he or she will quickly give you a list of others you would likely enjoy also. Nothing pleases librarians more than sharing the books they love. Novelist and critic Geoffrey O'Brien terms this "a reunion of old acquaintances" in his book *The Browser's Ecstasy: A Meditation on Reading*:

> Books went from hand to hand among us. With the exchange of a book many a love affair had begun; with a sudden change of opinion about the merits of a particular book had been signaled many a rupture of relations. . . . Through books we felt we lived multiple existences not previously our own. . . . To talk about those books, those lives, was a further interweaving that made them even more profoundly part of us.[3]

Shakespearean scholar Harold Bloom calls this "the reader's sublime" in his book *How to Read and Why*, his tribute to the ability of authors to create a kind of rapture in their readers. He believes that we read for any number of reasons: "that we cannot know enough people profoundly enough; that we need to know ourselves better; that we require knowledge, not just of self and others, but the way things are." Bloom maintains that the great novels of Jane Austen and Charles Dickens will "survive our ongoing Information Age, and not just as film or television." He is certain that we will go on reading *Emma* and *Great Expectations* because these novels "appeal to our childlike need for love, and recovery of self. . . . The 'why' of reading it is then self-evident: to go home again, to heal our pain."[4]

Each of us enjoys reading for many different reasons. Nancy Pearl, Seattle librarian, NPR book reviewer, and model for the popular librarian action figure, calls her love of books and reading "book lust," the title of her guide to good reading:

> Reading has always brought me pure joy. I read to encounter new worlds and new ways of looking at our own world. I read to enlarge

my horizons, to gain wisdom, to experience beauty, to understand myself better, and for the pure wonderment of it all. . . . I read for company, and for escape. . . . I read to meet myriad folks and enter their lives—for me, a way of vanquishing the "otherness" we all experience.[5]

After all those years of complaining that we have to buy the newest Danielle Steel, the next saccharine Nicholas Sparks novella, yet another vampire love story, another tell-all posthumous biography of Princess Di or Jackie O, or the latest overpriced and overhyped pop psychology book, selectors of core titles are liberated from purchasing books solely on the basis of client demand and now are free to make selections based on the quality of the considered title. It is a sad commentary on the state of selection in our libraries today that buying books for core collections on the basis of their merit is the exception rather than the rule.

One would expect that librarians would jump at the opportunity to buy only the very best books, but ironically this is not always the case. This freedom can be quite intimidating to selectors. It assumes that they have the book knowledge and subject expertise to make good core collection decisions. In libraries where high circulation has been touted as the measure of success and signals their importance to the community, allocating resources for books that might not circulate as often as best-sellers can be a frightening prospect to library administrators—one they may not be comfortable endorsing. The possible political implications of creating a core collection need to be addressed and understood by any library before it undertakes an extensive core collection development project.

During my years as collection development coordinator for the Phoenix Public Library, I worked with good, poor, and occasionally excellent selectors. The one thing they all had in common is that they thought they were doing a fine job selecting materials. Most librarians believe that the selection of materials is the profession's number-one inalienable right. As William Katz put it in his classic *Collection Development: The Selection of Materials for Libraries* (a definite core candidate in library literature), "The whole concept of professionalism is tested on the selection battle line."[6] In many library systems, the Phoenix Public Library included, selection is the one area that only the professional librarian is deemed capable of handling.

Library science is not a pure science, and the selection of library materials is even less so. Katz divides those who work as selector librarians into two groups:

> One group strongly involved with books and other print materials resists any effort to make a science of selection. For them selection is an almost intuitive process whereby the expert knows what is best for the community served. . . . At the other extreme are the "library scientists" who endeavor to objectify the whole selection process.

This group's argument is that, given enough data, a model can be constructed whereby selection may be predetermined.[7]

Katz feels that most librarians fall somewhere between the two philosophies. Although I agree with him, I think the profession as a whole would prefer to be thought of as scientists—"professionals"—rather than as artists using an intuitive selection system. It is telling that no library school offers a degree in the "Art of Librarianship." Wherever your personal philosophy falls between these two selector groups, the artist or the scientist, the ultimate battleground between selectors when considering whether to develop a core collection is the issue of "quality versus demand." Does the selector choose books "that will develop and enrich the lives of the persons being served by the library," materials to be selected from "deeper life channels"? Or does selection occur "in response to and in anticipation of demand"?[8] Put another way, selection can be based either on the bibliographic importance of a title within its own field or on its potential demand by library users. In a perfect world with unlimited resources of both funds and space, a library can consider buying on the basis of both criteria. Unfortunately, this is rarely possible.

A library must carefully weigh the quality-versus-demand issue before it can begin to develop a core collection. First, it must decide which side of the selection controversy it wishes to pursue. Ultimately this decision need not be as strictly defined as it might first appear, as long as the library staff can agree with one basic premise—that well-selected core titles will circulate. Although any one core title may not circulate initially as much as a current best-seller, its shelf life may ultimately prove longer over the years. The important thing to always keep in mind, no matter your personal selection preference, is that a core title that never goes out only gathers dust on a library shelf and will not enrich the life of any library user. For this reason, a less superior book might occasionally be designated a core title, on the basis of its readability and user appeal.

When you are undertaking any collection development work, you must understand that the art of selection is quite idiosyncratic and, therefore, can be very subjective. The core selections of your colleagues will most likely astonish you, as your core picks will surprise them. So to be fair to your coworkers and, even more important, to your community, it is crucial that you understand your inner librarian and what she or he ultimately brings to the selection arena. As anyone who has taken a library science class on selection or who has read any of the literature on the subject knows, one of the cardinal rules of collection development is to be impartial, to avoid purchases based on your personal interests, prejudices, religious beliefs, or opinions—your inner librarian, if you will. Core selection is quite possibly the only exception to this rule. Libraries will find that many of their librarians have well-developed interests that can greatly improve the quality of core title selection. The creation of a library's core collection is one of the few tasks where staff members' knowledge, expertise, hobbies, and avocations can be extremely valuable resources. These qualities, along with the usual selection tools of reviews, bibliographies, book lists, publishers' catalogs, websites, and personal examination, should be taken into account. It is crucial that each individual's knowledge be tapped and incorporated into the core creation process. This might prove difficult for those selectors who consider collection development a science, those who depend heavily on community analysis and statistical review of the collection to assist them in selection. Those of you who regard selection as an art must always understand that this process will be far more difficult for the scientists among us to accept.

Development of a core collection assumes that "the province and purpose of the public library is to provide for every person the education obtainable through reading. . . . It implies the use of books for spiritual and intellectual as well as for material and vocational profit, books for mental resources, reading for individual and personal joy." Helen Haines wrote this in 1935 (second edition, 1950), and some might argue that public libraries were more crucial seventy years ago because so few resources were available for continuing education. Public colleges were far more limited than today. There were very few community colleges, certainly no self-interest classes, and, hard as it might be to fathom, no Oprah book club. For many people, particularly women and immigrants, the library was essentially the only avenue open for continuing their education. Few today, however, would dispute the idea that basic library service still revolves around getting the "right book to the right reader. Without a reader a book is in suspended animation; without users a library is dead. People and books are the positive and negative poles that keep alive the current of library service."[9]

In its 2007 publication *To Read or Not to Read: A Question of National Consequence*, the National Endowment for the Arts stresses the importance of reading for our nation and how reading

> transforms the lives of individuals—whatever their social circumstances. Regular reading not only boosts the likelihood of an individual's academic and economic success . . . but it also seems to awaken a person's social and civic sense. Reading correlates with almost every measurement of positive personal and social behavior. . . . The cold statistics confirm something that most readers know but have mostly been reluctant to declare as fact—books change lives for the better.[10]

THEORIES OF THE SELECTION PROCESS

Much has been written on the process of developing library collections and writing selection statements, but very little actually specifies what criteria a selector needs to consider in deciding whether a title should be added to a library's collection. Additionally, today's library literature includes a wealth of material outlining the numerous steps that a library should take in designing its own particular selection process. There are many excellent guides to assist you in what can become a very involved selection process (several are included in chapter 6). These guides should prove helpful as you begin to develop everyday procedures for your library's collection development work. This book focuses on the philosophy of selection and gives you the tools you need to make knowledgeable selection decisions as they relate to the development of core collections. Discussions of procedures and processes here concentrate on the steps needed specifically to create high-quality core collections.

A few authors who are well known for their selection theories deserve special notice here. G. Edward Evans, former librarian of Harvard University's Tozzer Library, in his *Developing Library and Information Center Collections* gives a fine historical overview of the major writings on book selection and collection development from 1925 to 1981, and his book is a good starting point for additional reading. Evans's summary of eleven classic writers on the selection process includes S. R. Ranganathan, who in 1952 wrote *Library Book Selection*. Ranganathan's philosophy, as summarized by his five laws of librarianship, can be considered the cornerstone of developing a core collection—one that is of value to and well utilized by the community served by its library:

1 | Books are for use.

2 | Every reader his book.

3 | Every book its reader.

4 | Save the time of the reader.

5 | A library is a growing organism.[11]

All the authors whose theories Evans presents give practical advice to assist a librarian in general selection. Several of them make valuable points that are still of significance and can prove helpful for both the novice and the experienced core selector.

Francis Drury, in his 1930 textbook *Book Selection*, takes the "position that the value of a book is the basic reason to include it in a collection." Evans summarizes Drury's philosophy as follows: "the best quality reading material for the greatest number of patrons at the lowest possible price." We can all agree with this generalization. Drury also sets forth a series of selection guidelines to choose these "best" books, which for our purposes I call core titles. Among Drury's criteria is a personal favorite of mine: "Apply the Golden Rule in selecting books." Other suggestions include "Establish suitable standards for judging all books"; "Stock the classics and 'standards' in attractive editions"; "Be broad-minded and unprejudicial in selection; represent all sides fairly"; "Know authors and their works—if possible develop a ranking system"; and

"Do not attempt to complete sets, series, or subject areas unless there is actual demand for completeness."[12]

Evans also includes Helen Haines's classic, *Living with Books*, in his selection theory summary. Haines makes some excellent points that are quite appropriate for core collection creation:

> Select books that tend toward the development and enrichment of life. . . . Make the basis for selection positive, not negative. Every book should be of service, not simply harmless. . . . Select some books of permanent value regardless of their potential use; great library works must remain the foundation of the library's structure. . . . Strive not for a "complete" collection, but for the "best": the best books on a subject, best books of an author, most useful volumes of a series. . . . Prefer an inferior book that will be read over a superior one that will not.[13]

Evans concludes his overview chapter on the theories of the selection process with his own advice on how to become a first-rate book selector: "Be interested in what is going on in the world, and read, read, read!"[14]

Many of these excellent points are incorporated into the core collection statement for in-house staff use that we develop later in this chapter. Whether you agree with all these statements or not, they provide an excellent starting point for core list creation and staff discussions on the theories of the core selection process.

The extensive list of selection criteria Evans compiled includes several suggestions that are useful for general selection but do not work for core collection development. For example, Evans discusses Lionel R. McColvin, who Evans claims was one of the first to write a major text on book selection. In *The Theory of Book Selection for Public Libraries*, published in 1925, McColvin suggests that "the book should be complete and properly balanced," and, further, "the currency of the information is frequently the determining factor. . . . the writing style and treatment of the subject should be appropriate to the type of demand to be met."[15] Although at first glance these criteria appear to be admirable goals, they do not always work when applied to core selection. Quite often a core title is unique, and it is this very element that sets it apart, that makes it a classic and, therefore, a likely core candidate.

The historical perspective an author brings to his work can be the most significant aspect of a book and the very reason that it is of importance today, whether or not some of the ideas are still current or even accurate. Perhaps in the case of historical writing, additional information has come to light. One example that immediately comes to mind, perhaps the most prejudicial volume ever written, is Adolf Hitler's *Mein Kampf*. Other examples of core titles that fly in the face of McColvin's advice are Dee Brown's *Bury My Heart at Wounded*

Knee: An Indian History of the American West, Evan S. Connell's *Son of the Morning Star: Custer and the Little Bighorn,* Basil Davidson's much-disputed classic *Africa in History: Themes and Outlines,* or *Coming of Age in Samoa* by the currently out-of-favor (yet again) anthropologist Margaret Mead.

Certain styles of writing are difficult for the average reader, but this should not affect a title's inclusion in a core collection. Difficulty of reading is not a consideration because demand is not the deciding factor. Such works as Shakespeare's plays, Freud's *Interpretation of Dreams, Beowulf,* and Goethe's *Faust* would all be appropriately included in any core list, even though they are not particularly easy reading. These examples demonstrate the importance of a well-written core selection statement for staff that outlines the inclusion criteria for a core title. Unquestionably, such a statement needs to be established before you begin core collection development work.

COLLECTION DEVELOPMENT POLICY STATEMENTS

There are two distinct types of collection development policy statements, one written for the general public and the other a working document for in-house use by staff. You may encounter these statements labeled as collection development policy statements or as selection policy statements, a title currently less in vogue. Once there were differences between these two documents, but an examination of current library literature reveals that these two names are now used interchangeably. This can be confusing because there is no consistent nomenclature to differentiate between the two types of policy statements and determine whether they are being written for public or staff use. It is crucial that library staff determine the type of statement they are planning to write and who exactly they are addressing, regardless of what it is ultimately called. In this book I use the more common term, *collection development policy statement,* and attempt always to clarify the purpose of the policy statement and its intended user.

Collection Development Policy Statement as Mission Statement

One type of collection development statement is essentially an elaborate mission statement providing basic information about the scope of the library. It explains to the public, in a very general way, why the library has certain titles in its collection and not others. In essence it is a public relations document that often offers a quite grandiose overview of the library's mission; sometimes it incorporates a few standard goals. This general collection development statement is often coupled with the Library Bill of Rights and the ALA's Freedom to Read and Freedom to View statements. These three vital declarations can then be approved by your library's advisory board and included in your library's collection development statement. Because they express the basic principles of selection in a succinct and proficient manner, each of these documents can prove useful when responding to the public's concerns about why certain items are included in the library's collection and others are not. They carry the authority of the ALA, which adds clout to your statement. Freedom to View, for example, can be quite helpful when answering the public's queries about why videos or other audiovisuals are not rated and labeled to prevent young people from viewing "inappropriate" material. The Freedom to View statement explains this clearly, stating in no uncertain terms that libraries will resist "the constraint of labeling or prejudging film, video, or other audiovisual materials on the basis of the moral, religious or political beliefs of the producer or film maker or on the basis of controversial content."

The Phoenix Public Library's first "Materials Selection Statement" included all three ALA statements and the library's mission statement. The library's mission statement was barely three pages long and full of "marvelous" sentiments about the library's mission and the importance of the library to the citizens of Phoenix, echoing the ALA's philosophy as expressed in the Library Bill of Rights and the two Freedom documents. For example, this early Phoenix Public Library policy stated:

> The Phoenix Public Library strives to fill the informational, recreational and educational needs of our users, and to encourage non-users to partake of our services. We continually try to find ways to expand our services to more people, so that we can serve every possible kind of library user. In this effort, we provide materials old and new, classic and ephemeral, orthodox and unorthodox, in many media. . . . The Library will, within the limits of budget and general selection standards, select representative materials espousing divergent, avant-garde, and unusual points of view.

The last sentence is a particularly useful statement that I often, as the collection development coordinator, quoted when replying to the public's concerns about items in the library's collection. The Phoenix Public Library's selection statement and the three ALA statements were approved by its library advisory board in 1984. Board approval gives credibility to your policy statement and signifies its importance to your library and its community.

Our policy and the three ALA documents were printed in a slick pamphlet format, and copies were included with all our replies to collection concern queries. This pamphlet was then also used to answer general questions about the library's collection and was given to our users whenever they asked that recurring question: "Just how do you select your books anyway?" The complete text of the library's selection statement appeared in the *Librarians Collection Letter* newsletter of November 1993, and the ALA sold copies of it to requesting libraries across the country—an unexpected source of money for the Phoenix Public Library Education Fund.

A general mission statement is usually so unspecific and timeless that it does not need revision often, although it should be reread by every selector at least once a year and be readily accessible to selectors whenever a collection development question arises. The Phoenix Public Library's statement was recently reworked for the first time, almost thirty years after it was issued. Quotable and impressive as this type of policy document might be as a public relations instrument, it actually supplies little practical assistance to the librarian attempting to select titles; this responsibility lies with the policy statement as buying plan.

Collection Development Policy Statement as Buying Plan

More relevant to this book is the type of collection development policy statement that provides a plan with detailed guidelines for librarians concerning what exactly they are to select. "A policy statement is a document representing a plan of action and information, that is used to guide the staff's thinking and decision making; specifically the policy is consulted when considering in which subject areas to acquire material and deciding how much emphasis each area should receive." Importantly, it provides "a framework within which individuals can exercise their own judgment. . . . Without written statements the divergence of opinion can be confusing; with a policy statement everyone has a central reference point. Differences in opinion can be discussed with some hope that a basic understanding, if not agreement, can be reached."[16] I discuss the specific details of what should be included in this collection development policy later in this chapter.

More libraries than ever before are employing collection policy statements of one sort or another. There are many practical and intellectual reasons for writing this specific and detailed collection statement, but the most important is that it enables practicing librarians to know exactly what their administrators, supervisors, and collection development managers expect of them. It enables selectors to work with uniformity toward the goals and objectives outlined in the collection policy. It ultimately creates a selection manual that establishes continuity of process, making it easier for new staff to understand what their predecessors were trying to accomplish. In summary, such a policy statement can perform the following functions, as outlined clearly and succinctly by Evans:

1 | It informs everyone about the nature and scope of the collection.

2 | It informs everyone of collecting priorities.

3 | It forces thinking about organizational goals to be met by the collection.

4 | It generates some degree of commitment to meeting organizational goals.

5 | It sets standards for inclusion and exclusion.

6 | It reduces the influence of a single selector and personal biases.

7 | It provides a training/orientation tool for new staff.

8 | It helps ensure a degree of consistency over time and despite staff turnover.

9 | It guides staff in handling complaints.

10 | It aids in weeding and evaluating the collection.

11 | It aids in rationalizing budget allocations.[17]

Katz, in *Collection Development: The Selection of Materials for Libraries*, outlines some additional benefits. A written collection development statement can

1 | Assist in establishing methods of reviewing materials before purchase.

2 | Help in determining the best method of acquisition—directly from the publisher or through a jobber, for example.

3 | Offer some help against censorship by a clear statement of the type of materials to be purchased and indication that the policy has the support of the ruling body of the library.

4 | Help in long-range budget planning by stating priorities and outlining growth and development goals.

5 | Assist in planning with other libraries such cooperative programs as interlibrary loans and networks.

6 | Offer suggestions for what types of materials are to be weeded, stored, or discarded.[18]

Unlike the collection development statement as mission statement, this detailed and practical policy statement needs to be reviewed and updated on a regular basis if it is to retain its value for the staff. As a rule, this document is intended for in-house use only. In addition to its slickly published mission statement pamphlet, the Phoenix Public Library also had an elaborate scheme of almost one hundred collection development policy statements. These were written by the Central Library subject specialists for each of their subject areas. Upon approval they were signed by the library director, then sent to every library agency. This way every selector in the Central Library knew exactly what his or her selection responsibilities were. The statements also served as a reference point to assist librarians in the branches in understanding the Central

Library's collection goals and the parameters within which their branch selections must fall. Each statement clearly defined the subject area for the purpose of clarifying selection responsibility, and it listed the strengths of the subject area and its target groups. Subject specialists also supplied a list of the best and most useful sources of collection development information for their subjects. Another section listed additional information that the subject specialists felt would be important to pass along regarding their selection area—whether duplicate copies were ever purchased, periodical and approval plan information, storage and deselection considerations, and so forth.

The subject policy statements were written for every subject area in the Central Library. A lengthy general branch statement outlining the specific parameters for each of the general Dewey call numbers was prepared. Several branch selection policies were also written to explain how specific branch collections differed from other branch collections. Every one of these detailed collection development policy statements was reviewed on a three-year cycle and updated as warranted. Each review took almost an entire year. The current selector did the initial rewrite, which was reviewed by the immediate supervisor. Together with the appropriate administrator, they then met with the collection development manager and the library director to discuss the proposed changes to the selection document and the general state of the subject area's collection. The budget allocation for this subject was reexamined at the same time. This was an excellent way for selectors to discuss the goals and needs for their particular subject area directly with their supervisors and the library director.

If your library does not yet have a general collection development policy statement and you are anxious to begin creating a core collection, writing a statement that deals only with core titles might prove an excellent place to start. Because a core collection is finite and limited and remains constant longer than the rest of the general collection, it may prove easier for staff to tackle. Because most librarians have definite opinions on what is a "great book," the writing of a core policy should make for some lively staff discussions while letting staff air concerns about collecting the classics and simultaneously answering questions about core procedures and policies. It cannot be overemphasized that staff should have this important discussion opportunity and that a core collection policy statement should be available to refer to as librarians begin to create a core collection.

There are several practical handbooks on writing collection development policy statements as well as several extremely useful compilations of policy statements from various libraries around the country. Katz's classic *Collection Development* is an excellent resource, as is the ALA's *Guide for Written Collection Policy Statements* (1996), one of the association's excellent, easy-to-follow collection management guides. These are included in the annotated bibliography that appears in chapter 6. Although some of these titles may prove helpful in the writing of collection policy statements, none of them deals specifically with the singularities of core collection development. Remember this if you use these resources, and also establish at the outset your purpose in writing a library selection statement and your intended audience. Searching online can also provide access to collection development policies, for many libraries now make them available that way as well.

Realizing that there are almost as many ways to plan to write a collection development statement as there are libraries, in this chapter I present the specifics of a core selection statement, along with a sample policy document, figure 2.1 (below). The basic elements to think about as you confront the internal planning process for your library are outlined succinctly in *Developing Public Library Collections, Policies, and Procedures* by Kay Ann Cassell and Elizabeth Futas, which is part of the practical How-to-Do-It Manuals for Libraries series edited by Bill Katz. Additional collection development statements can be found in Elizabeth Futas's extremely helpful compilation *Collection Development Policies and Procedures*. In her introduction, Futas outlines the four components of the policy development process:

1 | Setting down exactly what is to be accomplished in a "planning to plan" group,

2 | Collecting the type and amount of information to make correct decisions,

3 | Formulating and writing the final document, and

4 | Determining what use is to be made of the final product—in other words, going from document to policy.[19]

A library must decide whether the planning process involves a group effort or one individual writing the core policy. Obviously there are pluses and minuses to either method. Anyone who has attempted to write with a group knows how difficult that can be. On the other hand, writing a policy in a vacuum without staff input can be the quickest way to doom any project. My suggestions are that you (1) establish a firm timetable for completion of the statement, (2) have one person be responsible for the writing, and (3) gather lots of input and review from the staff, advisory board, community groups, and library administration. Additional information on this whole "planning to plan" process can be located through the bibliography in chapter 6.

WRITING CORE COLLECTION DEVELOPMENT POLICY STATEMENTS

The primary purpose of writing a core collection development policy statement is to help library administrators and selector librarians "in the production of a document that serves as both a planning tool and communication device. The resulting policy statement should clarify collection development objectives to staff . . . and enable them to understand the collection, [and] anticipate what it may or may not contain."[20] Much of what has been published on writing collection development policy statements does not work for core collection development statements, for several reasons. Chief among them, as mentioned earlier, is that much of a core collection consists of titles that are unique; there are no strengths or weaknesses to build on, no areas to emphasize or to ignore—all core titles are created equal. There is no attempt at balance among subjects, no making sure that most subjects are covered uniformly. In many instances, there is even no concern that a title might be out of date. Remember that one of the definitions of a classic is that it is dateless and has stood the test of time.

A complete core collection encompasses all subject areas as well as the entire range of fiction writing, including the often-maligned science fiction, mystery, western, and romance genres. Generally there are no restrictions concerning what to include or exclude in a core collection on the basis of geographic area, copyright date, format, or circulation use. In creating a core collection, the selector is striving to find the best books available on a given topic or in a given genre. Therefore, this collection is considered to be "collection centered," meaning that core selection is accomplished in comparison to an external standard or bibliography.[21] For example, titles might be selected as core from some of the lists we have already mentioned: Hirsch's list of "What Literate Americans Know" that accompanied his *Cultural Literacy*; the Modern Library's list of the one hundred best books of the twentieth century; Oprah's Book Club titles; National Endowment for the Arts' Big Read suggestions; or the National Book Award winners. In chapter 3 I present criteria and specific selection tools to be used in creating core collections. It is important to remember at this point that core collections are "collection centered," whereas most general collections in public libraries are "use centered," with emphasis placed on the collection's use—how often and by whom. Although "use" is certainly of interest when you are developing core collections, it is never the primary concern. This is an important distinguishing feature of core collection development work.

Although the ALA, in its *Guide for Written Collection Policy Statements*, strongly recommends that the Pacific Northwest Conspectus approach to collection evaluation and description be used or at least adapted for most written policy statements, this is not useful for writing a core collection development policy. The Conspectus approach as defined in the ALA guide is a standardized "comprehensive survey; a tabulation of particulars representing a general view of them. The term as used here means an overview or summary of collection strengths and collecting intensities, arranged by subject, classification scheme, or a combination of either, and containing standardized codes for collection or collecting levels."[22] This method does not work well for core collections for the same reason mentioned earlier—because each title included in a core collection is equally important, there are no strengths or weaknesses within a core collection. The title either exists or it does not. The very nature of core collections lends itself much more naturally to the alternative to the Conspectus approach, what ALA terms in its guide to writing policy statements the "narrative statement."[23]

The type of narrative core statement I develop here is the collection development policy statement as buying plan. Its primary purpose is to be of assistance to core selectors. For our purposes, I assume that there already exists a general collection development policy statement written as a mission statement for use with the public. What follows is a basic outline for a core collection development policy statement accompanied by a brief description explaining the rudiments of each of the outline's components, much of which is discussed in greater detail in later chapters. There is certainly room for variation in the structure outlined here; it may differ from community to community. What is most important is that you use a structure that works for your library and your particular needs.

A core collection development policy statement should include most of the following sections:

1. *Introduction:* This brief section defines the purpose of this selection document and explains the mission of the core collection, its philosophy, its objectives and goals, and the principal target audience for the collection. Remember that there are differences between goals and objectives: goals are broad statements of intentions, whereas objectives are more specific and measurable and give details about how a goal is to be accomplished. If, for example, one of your goals is "to make the classics more accessible to the general public," your objective might be "to hold monthly great book discussions" or "to create reading lists." Objectives provide accountability for library staff, can be tied into their performance evaluations, and can be used to find out if your core collection mission is successful.

Some discussion of the potential users of the core collection and a brief analysis of the community the library serves should be included. This snapshot of the library's community might outline its ethnic makeup and religious affiliations and the projected population growth or decline along with the educational levels of the library's clientele. This information and other facts can be summarized from census tracts and local government reports. It is important to specify to what level of the community's readership you are directing core title selection. Sometimes the most important and definitive work on a subject is not accessible to the general public and a less superior, but more readable, title might better serve your clientele. If desired, at this point the statement can outline specific objectives for publicizing your new core collection, or it can simply mention that a core public relations plan will be implemented. The policy should clearly state if core titles are mandatory purchases for all library agencies.

2. *Definition of a core title and how it relates to the rest of the collection:* This is perhaps the most important aspect of your statement. It is crucial that staff

and their supervisors understand exactly what is meant by designating a book a "core title." This definition should also explain how the whole "classic" concept fits into the core collection's development.

3. *Statement regarding how core books are to be selected and who is responsible for their selection:* Selection procedures should be outlined and details provided on whether selection will be done by a committee, by individual librarians, by subject specialists, by community members, or outsourced to a library distributor. Procedures to be followed if the collection development policy statement itself needs to be revised or updated should be included. If you elect to duplicate the Phoenix Public Library's elaborate system of core forums, this needs to be spelled out as well.

4. *Criteria and guidelines used to select these titles:* This statement of criteria outlines the factors that contribute to making a book a core title. Factors might include that the title is a prize winner or the author of historical importance or great renown in a particular field. Other factors to consider are that the title is a groundbreaking work or, in the case of fiction, of great literary merit or has stood the test of time. Guidelines might include that a core title must be of continuing interest to the community and circulate a minimum of three times in any given year.

Specific guidelines should be written to include the particular interests and needs of your library's unique community. For example, because the Phoenix Public Library is located in the desert, we decided that gardening and landscaping core books must be written for our special climate even though superior titles exist for other and more general environments. It is helpful to specify the guidelines for including outstanding titles written about your city or state because finding reviews and bibliographic citations for area-specific titles can prove difficult. It is also important to discuss what types of materials you will not consider for the core—for example, foreign languages, workbooks, or college textbooks.

5. *Specific sources to be used in developing this collection:* Here you list the important bibliographies and book lists that you recommend selectors consult when searching for possible core titles. This section, if prepared carefully, is one of the most valuable and practical in helping selectors develop their core collections.

6. *Subject information:* It is doubtful that you will consider all subjects equally in the creation of core collections. We have already touched on the fact that geographic emphasis might be a determining factor for inclusion in a core collection. The demographics of Phoenix suggest that novels dealing with American Indian or Hispanic cultures be given preference over novels that illuminate other cultures. With fiction, you might consider developing different criteria for a mystery book than for a general fiction title. It is virtually impossible to compare the literary excellence of the first lady of mysteries Agatha Christie to the "Great Books" of George Eliot or Henry James, but

certainly most would agree that Christie is a classic mystery writer and should be available in any size public library.

You might include suggestions on what to look for when selecting titles on different subject areas. Although much of core should stand the test of time and is therefore ageless, this is rarely the case with medical or technology books, for instance. You might decide to exclude such categories from the core entirely, recommend that they be reviewed more frequently than other subjects, or establish a totally different set of inclusion criteria.

7. *Formats included or excluded:* In addition to the usual paperback/hardcover decision, you must decide if your library is to have a core film collection or a collection of classic audiobooks or the best music or, alternatively, no alternate formats at all. If a library decides to include alternate formats in its core collection, specific details pertaining to these formats' selection, acquisition, and maintenance should be outlined in a separate section. Selectors also need to decide if a printed book is not really necessary if it is available in another format, such as video, audiobook, or e-book. In other words, would the unabridged audiobook, e-book, or film version of *The Three Musketeers* be sufficient? I am certainly not advocating such substitutions, just recommending that you consider the possibility, because funds and space are almost always at a premium in libraries.

8. *Budget considerations:* Although it would be wonderful if budget did not play a major role in selection, this is never the case. Your library must decide exactly how much money is to be devoted to developing a core collection knowing that, in most cases, money will have to be taken from somewhere else to cover core expenditures. It must be understood that, if the same number of core titles is required to be purchased by every branch no matter its size, core title expenditures will eat up a larger proportion of a smaller budget than a larger one. Library systems that have floating collections, in which titles do not have a specific branch home, must decide who pays for core titles. Similarly, you must decide who pays for core e-books that are used systemwide. Library systems that have centralized selection or distributors selecting their core books must include a list of these titles in the library's profiles. Today libraries have many options for selecting and purchasing titles, so each library has to work to determine the best method for incorporating core selections in its budget. Allocation of funds is always a true indicator of a library's priorities. Before embarking on creating a core collection, the powers that be must all be in agreement that the core is an important facet of your library's collection and will be funded adequately. Additional funding sources, such as grants, need to be considered and factored into budget planning for core collections.

9. *Out-of-print material:* When the first edition of this book was written, purchasing out-of-print titles was an expensive and labor-intensive process for libraries. Happily, this is no longer the case. Today out-of-print titles can be purchased easily and quickly, through web vendors such as Amazon and Alibris,

often at a lower price than when the book was first released (see chapter 4). Once Google Book Search becomes more usable and e-readers become widespread, they both will provide additional affordable ways to obtain core titles that are out of print. Additionally, some may be available for free downloading from online book catalogs, such as Project Gutenberg, the oldest digital library. With increased digitization of titles in the public domain, more and more out-of-print core titles will become readily available, and ultimately whether a core title is out of print will become unimportant—a nonissue.

10. *Impact on technical services:* Core procedures need to be reviewed with the library's technical services department because selections in addition to an already established buying cycle—including possible out-of-print title purchases, new core budget levels, and special processing or cataloging to designate a core title—all have an impact on technical services' workflow. Technical services staff should be involved in any core decision that has ramifications for their work. Potential problems can be avoided if your catalogers as well as processing and acquisitions staff understand what the library is trying to accomplish by establishing a core collection.

11. *Collection maintenance—replacement and deselection:* Procedures need to be established for ensuring that your core collection titles are replaced as condition or loss warrants. This might be done most expediently on a regular cycle so that specific titles are available for order only once a year. This approach saves individual librarians from having to check their shelves for core titles and ordering the same title repeatedly throughout the year, making additional work for them and the technical services staff. The impact of replacement on the materials budget must also be considered, since yearly ongoing replacement can be costly. Procedures for how a title is to be deleted or added to a core list must be explained here if you wish to maintain consistency in core collections throughout the library system.

12. *Evaluation—updating and core collection review:* Core titles need to be reviewed on a regular basis to see if they have been circulating and whether they continue to retain importance for your community. Core lists need to be examined on a regular cycle to determine if there are new titles to be added and others to be deleted. A detailed schedule review plan makes certain this evaluation is repeated regularly enough to ensure that core collections remain viable and useful.

Publishers' catalogs, lists, and websites need to be examined to see if any core title has come back into print or if a new edition of a standard work has been released that might now be considered for core purchase—for example, Nobel laureate Seamus Heaney's recent translation of the Anglo-Saxon epic *Beowulf,* or the new highly acclaimed and extremely readable translations of Tolstoy's *War and Peace* and *Anna Karenina* by Richard Pevear and Larissa Volokhonsky.

13. *Selector performance:* When a core committee's work has been completed and the core selection list issued, selectors should be evaluated on their

core selection decisions and participation during committee meetings and core forums. Selectors need to be informed in a timely manner how well they did their job and supervisors told about the quality of their employees' core work. Ideally, core selection should be a factor in a librarian's yearly performance evaluation. Outlining the selector review process in the core policy statement ensures that selectors know that their core work will be evaluated and their job performance rated.

After the core selection policy has been written, it should be approved by the library administration and a copy issued to every agency systemwide. The writing of a collection development policy statement is time consuming, and not even the best statement reflects all the nitty-gritty details that go into the complicated process of daily core collection work. Not everyone will be pleased with this statement. This is to be expected. The most important goal of any policy statement is that it be a working document that is used by selectors.

Selectors need to be aware of the core selection policy, and every staff member involved in core collection work must have access to this document at all times. Ideally each selector will have a copy readily available. Large libraries may consider having every selector sign an affirmation that he or she has read the policy and understands it. Remember that the core selection policy statement needs to be reevaluated at least once a year, along with the entire core collection concept. Time consuming, certainly, but a necessary step to maintain the integrity of the entire core project.

SAMPLE CORE COLLECTION DEVELOPMENT POLICY STATEMENT

The policy statement shown in figure 2.1 was written for the fictional Southwest Public Library system as a model that libraries can use to develop their own core collections. This statement is intended as a buying plan for core materials and can be adapted to meet the unique needs of a specific library's clientele. This sample document assumes that the library already has a general collection development policy statement that was written as a mission statement (as explained earlier in this chapter) and can be used as a public relations document as needed. For the purposes of this book, standard sources useful in developing core collections are listed and annotated in chapter 6. In practice, selectors may want to add these sources directly into their selection policy statements. Additional subject-specific bibliographies can be found in the introductory notes that precede each of the core lists created for this book (chapter 7).

FIGURE 2.1

THE SOUTHWEST PUBLIC LIBRARY'S CORE COLLECTION DEVELOPMENT POLICY STATEMENT

Introduction

The Southwest Public Library has experienced one of the most dramatic growth rates of any city in the United States. The library serves a diverse population comprising a broad spectrum of cultural and ethnic backgrounds. The library strives with its core collection to provide the very best and most significant titles for its adult users. A core title is defined as being "of the highest quality, class, and rank."

The intent of this document is to give guidance and direction to library staff for the collection development, selection, and maintenance of the adult core circulating collection. This collection consists of a stringent selection of high-quality works of fiction and nonfiction titles on a wide range of subjects that span the entire Dewey range, 001–999. Additionally, the collection will contain representative audiovisual materials that meet similar standards of excellence, including films and music. Every core title must be available for circulation in every branch and the central library.

Purpose

The primary purpose of the core collection is to provide in each branch and the central library the seminal works of literary and historical renown that have been critically acclaimed as definitive in their respective fields. These titles must be of the highest quality and must in every instance appeal to and be used by the clientele of the library. The core collection will reflect the rich diversity of cultures that make up the library's community and the nation as a whole, along with regional titles of particular interest to the library's users.

Philosophy

The library's core collection makes no attempt to be well rounded or complete, but rather to supply only the best fiction and the best-written nonfiction available on a wide range of subjects that will interest and prove accessible to the educated layperson. Materials are selected for the core collection on the basis of their ability to enrich the lives of library users. The Southwest Public Library strives through its core collection to become a People's University providing titles of value for the lifetime learner.

Selection

Under the direction of the collection development coordinator, selectors will identify titles for inclusion in the library's core collection. Staff will seek information about core titles using standard bibliographies, review media, and their own critical judgment. Additionally, selectors will seek the opinion of local experts in the community. Each designated core title will undergo a rigorous selection process, including discussion at an open forum and administrative approval. These materials are selected on the basis of their accessibility to the educated layperson, their outstanding quality, and the selecting librarian's confidence that each title should be in every branch of the Southwest Public Library and is most likely to be in every public library's collection, including branch and small-town libraries.

Every adult services librarian will be given a yearly core assignment and will be responsible for completing it on schedule. Participation in committee meetings and forums is mandatory. Core selection work will be evaluated by the collection development coordinator, who will complete a core selector performance evaluation on each core committee member. Core selectors will be given a copy of their evaluation within one month of a core list's approval, and a copy will also be sent to their immediate supervisor and appropriate administrator. Core work will be factored into a selector's yearly performance evaluation.

General Criteria

Each core title must be considered on its own intrinsic merits. There is no single standard that can be applied in all cases when making the decision to include a title in the library's core collection. Among the general criteria that selectors should consider are

Critical acclaim and awards

Inclusion in special lists and standard bibliographies

Readability and clarity

Current and historical value

Reputation and significance of the author

Insight into the human condition

Importance as a social document

Timeliness

Quality of writing

Relevance to the community

Level of treatment

When necessary, core committee members will develop specific core criteria for individual subject areas. Selectors will also identify key subject-specific bibliographic sources for their assigned subjects; these references will be cited in the final core list.

Collection Maintenance

The library realizes the need to evaluate the core collection to ensure that its titles continue to be of value and significance to the community. The collection will be reviewed in an ongoing three-year cycle to determine whether each title continues to be the best title available for the library's users. On occasion titles may be removed from the core collection for various reasons: the material is no longer of historical importance, its reputation has slipped, or its annual circulation is fewer than five times. Removal of a core designation must be approved by the collection development coordinator and in most instances will be considered only during the appropriate subject review cycle. Titles withdrawn from the core collection may be moved to the general circulating collection, discarded, or given to the Friends group for the book sale. Materials that are worn, mutilated, or missing will be replaced in a timely manner.

The acquisitions staff will use online "bookstores" to search and purchase print books over the Internet along with secondary jobbers, whenever the library's primary vendor is not able to supply a required core title. Core titles will be labeled as such upon receipt and tagged with a core designation in the library online catalog. This designation will be removed globally whenever a title is removed from the core collection. This collection development policy statement and all core procedures will be reviewed yearly by the collection development coordinator with input from selectors.

Additional Notes

When a title is designated as core and a branch or the central library already has the title, this may become the core copy, but only if it is still in good condition. If not, a new copy must be purchased. If the existing copy is retained as core, it must be reprocessed as a core title.

If available, hardcover editions of core titles will be purchased. Branches may purchase additional copies of any core title in paperback or hardcover, depending on the agency's needs. Core titles may be bought in the additional formats of audiobook or electronic book; however, these will not be purchased in place of the printed book. They are offered merely as a service to the library's users.

Core committees, under the direction of the collection development coordinator, will develop programs or create book lists to help publicize the core collection and the titles contained within it.

Initial core purchases for the entire Dewey range will be paid for from a central fund monitored by the collection development coordinator and approved by the administration. The core allocation will not exceed 10 percent of the entire adult materials budget. Subsequent purchases after the three-year cycle that are needed to update and maintain the core collection will be paid for from the individual branch's budget.

Final advice to selectors as they begin the core selection process: *When in doubt, just leave it out!*

Notes

1. Brenda Knight, *Women Who Love Books Too Much* (Berkeley: Conari, 2000), 1.
2. Quoted in Ronald B. Shwartz, ed., *For the Love of Books: 115 Celebrated Writers on the Books They Love Most* (New York: Grosset/Putnam, 1999), xvi.
3. Geoffrey O'Brien, *The Browser's Ecstasy: A Meditation on Reading* (Washington, D.C.: Counterpoint, 2000), 3–4.
4. Harold Bloom, *How to Read and Why* (New York: Scribner, 2000), 29, 165.
5. Nancy Pearl, *Book Lust: Recommended Reading for Every Mood, Moment, and Reason* (Seattle: Sasquatch Books, 2003), ix.
6. William A. Katz, *Collection Development: The Selection of Materials for Libraries* (New York: Holt, 1980), 4.
7. Ibid.
8. G. Edward Evans, *Developing Library and Information Center Collections*, 2nd ed. (Littleton, Colo.: Libraries Unlimited, 1987), 82–83.
9. Helen E. Haines, *Living with Books: The Art of Book Selection*, 2nd ed. (New York: Columbia University Press, 1950), 15, 16.
10. National Endowment for the Arts, *To Read or Not to Read: A Question of National Consequence* (Washington, D.C.: National Endowment for the Arts, 2007), 4.
11. For discussion of Ranganathan, see, e.g., Evans, *Developing Library and Information Center Collections*, 95–96.
12. On Drury, see, e.g., ibid., 86–88.
13. Haines quoted in ibid., 91–92.
14. Ibid., 104.
15. On McColvin, see ibid., 83–84.
16. Evans, *Developing Library and Information Center Collections*, 66.
17. Ibid., 67.
18. Katz, *Collection Development*, 19.
19. Elizabeth Futas, ed., *Collection Development Policies and Procedures*, 3rd ed. (Phoenix: Oryx, 1995), 4.
20. Bonita Bryant, ed., *Guide for Written Collection Policy Statements*, Collection Management and Development Guides, No. 3 (Chicago: American Library Association, 1989), 2.
21. Barbara Lockett, ed., *Guide to the Evaluation of Library Collections*, Collection Management and Development Guides, No. 2 (Chicago: American Library Association, 1989), 3.
22. Joanne S. Anderson, ed., *Guide for Written Collection Policy Statements*, 2nd ed., Collection Management and Development Guides, No. 7 (Chicago: American Library Association, 1996), 28.
23. Ibid., 9.

CHAPTER 3

SELECTING A CORE COLLECTION

In literature, as in love, we are aston-
ished at what is chosen by others.
—André Maurois

AFTER ALL THE LIBRARIAN selectors have had a chance to review the library's core collection policy statement thoroughly, it is time for librarians to put these procedures into practice and to implement goals and objectives as outlined in this collection document. They will discover almost immediately that this is not an easy, or enviable, task. Although all the selectors have had ample opportunity to ask questions and discuss this policy statement, it is fairly certain that, when they actually begin to develop their core collections, uncertainty and confusion will remain.

Selectors must reconcile themselves to the fact that they will make mistakes in choosing core titles. You may select titles that are not the best, miss valuable titles, pick titles that do not circulate, or choose titles that are discredited later (always embarrassing). These situations can be quite upsetting, because an erroneous core selection is magnified when multiplied throughout the entire library system; librarians are thrifty souls and hate to waste a single dollar of an always too small book budget. As a core selector you may feel that your entire reputation as a librarian is in question, that experienced selectors should know core titles and be able to pull these extraordinary books out of thin air. So be prepared—mistakes will be made, no matter how well you lay the groundwork.

At the Phoenix Public Library we created an elaborate process of committees and staff forums to ensure that elements of consistency spanned core selection within all subjects. Because we were demanding that every library agency purchase these recommended core titles with their own funds no matter their size or budget, we felt that branch representation and buy-in were paramount to ensure the success of this endeavor. (The policy did eventually change once we understood exactly how great a financial burden this requirement placed on some of the smaller branches.) In chapter 4, I discuss budget and funding considerations and how the Phoenix Public Library dealt with them.

At the outset of core collection development, we expected each branch to expend its budgetary monies to purchase any designated core titles that were not already held in its collections. This policy had the greatest impact on the smallest branches with limited budgets. Many of these smaller agencies with correspondingly smaller budgets were located in the inner city and often served a larger proportion of Hispanic users. Librarians in these branches wondered whether core titles would circulate and despaired of earmarking the funds in their materials budget to cover the cost. The Central Library staff, on the other hand, wondered why they needed a particular core title when they already had plenty of materials on the very same topic—in some cases, titles that were even more inclusive than a potential core title. For example, Central Library selectors questioned their need to purchase the core committee's recommended one-volume *Dr. Axelrod's Mini-Atlas of Freshwater Aquarium Fishes* when they already had a complete multivolume set about tropical fish along with Dr. Axelrod's original atlas, which included more than four thousand tropical fishes. But this new, single volume was better suited to a branch collection and the needs of the home hobbyist, and the Phoenix Public Library's policy was that, if it was appropriate for a branch library, it certainly was appropriate for the Central Library. Although the Central Library served a wide range of users throughout the city, it also functioned as a branch library for the people living in the immediate vicinity. We were also aware that, though the library system provided excellent daily courier service among all agencies, it was still likely that if a library user did not find a desired book on the shelf, he or she might not ask to reserve it from another branch

One of the guiding principles of nonfiction core selection is that a library patron may not have a particular title in mind but should always have the best books available on any given subject no matter the size of the library the patron is visiting. Librarians who are unfamiliar with a particular subject area would then be able to recommend a core title with the assurance that it was a superior choice for the patron.

We hoped that the stipulation of requiring purchase of every missing core title in the branch agencies and the Central Library would establish systemwide uniform core collections and intensify selector interest in the entire core process as well as ensure staff attendance at core forums and increase staff input during these subject forums. We wanted librarians to feel that they each had a stake in every title selected for the core collection. We believed this would result in the best core collection for the entire library system.

Everyone attending core forums was given the opportunity to vote on every title recommended for the core list and was able to suggest additional titles for inclusion. The only exception to this rule was that, whenever fiction titles were discussed, attendees were limited to voting only on those titles they had read, much like the Academy Awards where, for example, only actors are allowed to nominate other actors. Fiction committee members felt that staff were so universally well read in fiction that they could base informed core choices on their own personal reading rather than just using reviews or book lists. The fiction selectors still consulted bibliographies and reviews to avoid making choices solely on hearsay or judgmental opinions about the overall quality of best-sellers, such as *Gone with the Wind, The Thorn Birds, All the Pretty Horses,* or *Shōgun,* all of which were eventually included in the Phoenix Public Library's fiction core collection. During the forum discussion, however, a consensus vote for a novel by attendees who had read the book could vault it into the core collection despite its lack of critical acclaim, or vice versa. This staff override was most useful when we were selecting which of a classic author's two or three titles would appear in the core fiction collection. The fiction forums truly were a book lover's delight. I can still remember some of the more eloquent pleas along with the wheeling and dealing that went on as librarians worked to get their beloved titles designated as core.

At the Phoenix Public Library, we began the core selection process by dividing the entire Dewey range, including biography and fiction, into three fairly equal parts. The plan was that we would review every subject and the entire fiction collection for core collection creation by the end of a three-year period, after which the three-year cycle would begin all over again; we would review a third of the core collection yearly. The first go-around of the entire adult collection actually took four years. We devoted the first year to developing the procedures and schedules for core work. Then, over the next three years, we examined the entire collection and selection sources for potential core titles, core committees and forums met, and we issued core selection lists and ordered titles.

Committee participation was mandatory for all adult services librarians, and all were asked to select on which of the subject committees they wanted to serve. Interested technical services librarians as well as juvenile and young adult services librarians were invited to contribute. Some librarians requested their subject assignment preferences based on their areas of expertise; others directed their choices toward those subjects where they felt weakest and wanted to learn more. Each of the Central Library's subject specialists was required to serve on the core committees that covered his or her assigned selection areas. We felt that these specialists' subject knowledge was a vital resource that needed to be tapped for core collection development.

Several of the Central Library's librarians also elected to serve on additional committees in subject areas of particular interest to them. Core committee work was one of the few times that branch selectors and subject specialists worked together toward a common goal. Staff gained an appreciation of the difficulties inherent in each type of library work, and the core collections were ultimately stronger because of this selector mix.

Timetables and schedules were implemented, and core committee members worked diligently to select only the best titles, titles that they knew they would eventually have to justify to staff and library administrators at the open core forums. Drafts of the core lists were sent out to all librarians well in advance of the forums so they could review the recommended titles before the forum date. This enabled all staff members to make additions and deletions, even if they were unable to attend the forum meeting.

The decisions made at core forums would ultimately affect each agency's collections and budgets, so it was in the best interests of every agency to have its staff members attend. Making each member of every core committee defend her or his titles publicly at these staff forums produced quite a bit of staff angst, but it resulted in excellent and tightly controlled core lists. Staff quickly separated the wheat from the chaff when their funds were at risk. No one wanted to spend money on any title that was not deemed of the highest quality or would not circulate. All members of the particular committee whose list was being discussed, along with a representative from each branch and from the Central Library subject areas, were required to attend each forum. Library administrators and the library director usually attended, and agencies often sent several representatives—strength in numbers, I guess. Having the administrators attend forums along with staff clearly stressed the importance of core work in the Phoenix Public Library system.

We invited librarians from surrounding city libraries as well as schools and universities to attend the core forums. Many came and appeared to enjoy these lively discussions. We had occasionally consulted university librarians with specific subject expertise during the creation of some core lists. It was valuable and enlightening for staff to hear their academic colleagues' comments and suggestions. These university brethren were given another opportunity to discuss their specific core recommendations when they attended the library's subject forums. All of this made for some enlightening battles during forums as individual titles were presented by selectors, some of whom were better prepared than others to defend their titles.

The first core forum did not go well at all. The unfortunate committee members had no written criteria to follow, and the parameters seemed to change minute by minute during the actual forum. Understandably, the participants felt like guinea pigs. We quickly drew up extremely broad criteria, listing just a few basic points, before the next forum. This alleviated some of the stress of the first forum, but the hastily written criteria were still too unspecific and open to interpretation to prove of much help to core selectors. (This will, of course, not be the case in your library! Your core criteria will undoubtedly be clearly laid out in your core collection policy statement.)

Not all libraries, particularly smaller systems or single-agency libraries, will find it necessary to implement the elaborate process of committees and forums that we undertook in Phoenix. Be that as it may, I cannot stress enough that, whatever methods your library ultimately uses to develop and implement core collection creation, specific and detailed written criteria are of the utmost importance. It is significant to reiterate at this juncture just how much time we devoted to core collection development in Phoenix, clearly demonstrating again how important we considered selection and core collection development. Selector time and effort were expected, and librarians were evaluated yearly on their core collection work.

We developed a performance evaluation checklist and sent a copy to all core selectors before they began their yearly assignments, so they knew exactly what was expected of them. The performance checklist noted whether core selectors

1 | Met deadlines.

2 | Searched representative and assigned bibliographies.

3 | Analyzed circulation data and adjusted core lists accordingly.

4 | Reviewed Central Library subject areas and personally examined core selections.

5 | Attended committee meetings and forums and communicated effectively.

6 | Visited local bookstores.

7 | Consulted local community experts.

8 | Displayed a thorough knowledge of their assigned subject area.

9 | Recommended appropriate core titles.

10 | Completed order forms accurately.

11 | Developed a suitable core program or book list.

When the core list was finalized, the collection development coordinator completed this checklist within a month. A copy of the checklist was sent to each core selector and to the selector's supervisor and administrator for their review. Core selectors who did exceptional work were given personal commendations signed by the library director and, in some instances, were given bonus personal leave hours. There was never any doubt in any staff member's mind that core work was considered to be of the utmost priority for every single librarian.

This discussion of the core title process is intended to assist libraries of all sizes in beginning their core projects. Bear in mind as you create your own core procedures G. Edward Evans's valid point that "collection development was, is, and always will be a subjective, biased work. The interventions of a selector's personal values into the process can never be completely avoided."[1] The Phoenix Public Library's open staff forums and committee-created core lists were attempts to make the subjective work of collection development ultimately accountable to the entire library and to use selectors' considerable knowledge and "personal values" to create the best possible core collection.

BASICS OF CORE SELECTION

The guiding principle behind core collections is that the general public has needs for materials beyond the current best-sellers and ready-reference materials. It is thought that at some point during people's adult lives they will desire materials for what Helen Haines calls "deeper life channels," and this craving will "require lasting, high quality materials."[2] In *The Readers' Choice: 200 Book Club Favorites*, a marvelous list of reader-tested recommendations for book club reading, Victoria Golden McMains celebrates the joy of discovering book "treasures." "Something wonderful is happening to books. People are reading them. The American public, once accused of planting itself in front of the television, has spearheaded a rapidly growing movement in the form of reading groups. Oprah has one. National Public Radio has one. Every small bookstore can refer you to one. The Denver area alone has three hundred."[3] These book clubs are not choosing to read best-sellers; they are reading and discussing core titles and the classics. This is exactly what core selectors love to hear and ultimately what makes the entire core process worthwhile.

Two basic elements must always be considered during selection of core titles. One is the value or importance of the title, and the other is whether this title has an audience and will prove to be of use and interest to your community. William A. Katz uses the words *evaluation* and *selection* to denote these two factors. He suggests that librarians must "distinguish between evaluation and selection, knowing that even those materials rated highly on the evaluation scales might not always be appropriately selected for a particular collection." He explains further that "evaluation is judging the intrinsic merits of materials. Selection is determining whether the materials meet the needs of the individual users."[4] Although Katz is not talking about core selection, this two-pronged approach works quite well for core selection; it is important that selectors have their audience in mind and remember, as we stressed earlier, that a book that is not used is of no value to anyone.

There is always the danger of choosing core and classic titles that have received extraordinary reviews and are of breathtaking quality but that the general library user does not care to read. This is not to say that the average public library reader might not be interested in reading difficult tomes on a particular subject of interest but, rather, that books written by an academic in a specialized area might not hold universal appeal. The general user might occasionally seek an academic title, but it will most likely not attract the wider audience that we are searching for when designating a title as core. Although a public library certainly buys books written for the specialist, such titles, even though highly touted, need not be designated as core, thereby making them a mandatory systemwide purchase. Katz concludes his discussion on the two elements of collection work by saying that "ideally, evaluation and selection do not conflict; actually, they usually do not."[5] I have found this to be true: a fine nonfiction core title or a classic novel will have stood the test of time and will still have great merit and be of continuing interest to today's library users.

At the Phoenix Public Library we found, much to our surprise, that core titles often circulated more in our smaller collections than at the regional branches. Limited branch collection size and funding meant that there might very well be only one biography of Mozart or Charles Darwin on the shelves of a smaller branch, both of them core titles, while larger collections might have several biographies of these men. Often core titles plugged holes in collections that selectors had not recognized. One of our most surprising findings was that core philosophy books circulated extremely well systemwide, particularly in collections where no titles on this subject were previously available. Inner-city branch managers had always assumed that there would be limited or no interest in this fairly esoteric subject and that the few interested clients could order these titles from the Central Library. This finding demonstrates why it is extremely crucial that core selectors keep an open mind throughout the core selection process and never underestimate the public's love of learning, books, and reading.

Librarians no longer, if they ever truly did, have the luxury of physically examining every book before selecting titles for their collections. The huge amount of staff time this would take, along with the expense of purchasing review copies, space considerations, and the increased delay in receipt of titles (particularly for today's customer who wants the newest items yesterday), certainly precludes most public libraries from undertaking item-by-item review by their staff. Even more time consuming would be staff personally reading every single title before selection. Far-fetched as this ideal might sound, for core title selection it is recommended that staff personally examine each and every suggested core title before adding it to the subject core list.

Personally reviewing core candidates is not as impossible as it may at first appear. I am not talking about hundreds of titles per selector (see the sample core lists in chapter 7). A core committee member might be nominating only two or three titles for core designation within a particular Dewey range. It is only through personal examination that a selector can take a book for a "test drive" to determine its readability and accessibility as well as evaluate its overall "curb" appeal. It is a good idea to bring core candidates to the forum or establish a core title review area where librarians not working on a subject list can examine potential titles. Details on how to accomplish this daunting review task and make it time well spent follow later in this chapter.

In "By Your Selection Criteria Are Ye Known," Daniel T. Richards, collection development officer of the National Library of Medicine, provides an excellent outline of what he labels "generic selection criteria." He maintains that "these criteria form the basis for the selection process in any library. They apply to all materials but may assume a greater or lesser importance depending on the type of material under consideration. . . . The selection process should be a weighing of these factors, one against or with another, to reach a decision."[6]

Additionally, Richards's succinct outline of selection considerations, although created for a medical facility, provides helpful definitions when applied specifically to core title selection. One consideration is *use/need*, which I emphasize as of primary importance in selecting a core title. Richards also talks about *content/relevance* and *scope/audience level* as they pertain to the library's collection. These are extremely important considerations to balance when you are selecting core titles. I have already mentioned that, when selecting for a core collection, you are attempting to find the best books in any given subject. This is not, however, completely accurate. Although you are looking for the finest material available on a topic, it also must be accessible and understandable to the public library user or educated layperson. As Richards says, "Preference may be given to works which provide broader coverage of a topic" and "are of sufficient breadth to be of use and interest to a larger segment of the user group."[7] For example, although the best medical book may be *Cecil's Textbook of Medicine*, written for the medical practitioner, you would be more likely to include on your core list the *Merck Manual of Medical Information*, which was written specifically for the general public, rather than the superior but more difficult to comprehend textbook. In all instances core title selection must dovetail with the scope of the rest of your collection.

Katz recommends bearing in mind three key words when determining the appropriate reader for a particular book. These key words reflect the difficulty of the reading matter contained in the book: *popular, scholarly,* or *technical.*[8] The best way to determine reading level is for the librarian to examine the title under consideration and read a chapter or two to determine the intended audience and level of subject treatment. Although consulting reviews and recommended bibliographies is vital in identifying a title for core consideration, nothing takes the place of a librarian's personal hands-on evaluation.

It is important at this juncture to remind core selectors never to doubt the knowledge and interests of their library's clientele. The core title user is usually well read; core collections are created for the reading public. Such readers are, at the very least, highly motivated and are reading, as Harold Bloom says, "to strengthen the self and to learn."[9] This is not to say that a library should not have ESL materials or easy adult readers, just that core collections are not established to serve these segments of the public.

Richards also discusses the importance of quality in selection. He talks about two types: *content* and *technical* quality. For our purposes, content quality is of prime consideration when you are designating a title for core selection. "Content quality is best determined by weighing several subjective factors collectively. Those factors include sponsorship; the degree of scholarship; the lasting value of the item; the reputations of the author, publisher, the contributors, the editorial board, and the producers; the authority of the information presented; and the impact of the item in the field."[10] Technical quality as discussed by

Richards pertains more to the actual physical properties of the book, such as its paper and binding. Although important for extended public library use, these properties are not a primary consideration for core inclusion.

At the Phoenix Public Library we gave the following general statements to all core selectors to assist them in understanding what titles should be included in the core selection lists. The core list should include only books that meet all the following criteria:

1 | The content is accessible to the educated layperson.

2 | The quality of the work is outstanding.

3 | The topic is one in which there is at least some public interest.

4 | You, the selecting librarian, are confident that this book should be in every public library's collection, including branch libraries and small-town public libraries.

The following are *not* criteria sufficient to cause a book to be included on a core list:

1 | It is the best book available on its topic. (Unless a book is outstanding in its own right, it should not be included. If there is no outstanding book on a topic, then that topic need not be represented in the core list. Comprehensive coverage or collection balance are not the purposes of these lists.)

2 | Popular demand for the book or the topic is high. (Books of marginal or mediocre quality will not be included simply because they are popular.)

. . . and remember, when in doubt, just leave it out!

Mandatory purchase of core titles for all branches and the central library is a crucial component of the entire core selection process. If your library chooses not to require purchase of every title designated as core, the importance of these titles is ultimately negated. If budget funds are allocated solely on the basis of a library's circulation, which is the case in far too many libraries, there is even less incentive for librarians to purchase core titles that admittedly will not circulate as much as best-sellers. Selectors must be assured at every opportunity that purchasing core titles will not result in a budget reduction for their agencies.

Without required purchase of core titles, selectors do not feel strongly about buying core titles. There is no impetus for them to do so. In such a case, core selection lists become little more than add and replacement lists, and there is no upgrading of your library's collections. Although well-chosen core titles admittedly make fine replacement selection lists, there is no certainty that staff will agree to purchase every one of these titles of their own volition.

SELECTION AIDS

Librarians selecting titles for inclusion in a library's collection have a tremendous variety of resources to assist them in making collection development choices: reviews, national bibliographies, subject lists, award winners, and "best of" lists. Within each of these categories the choices are overwhelming, and selectors universally recognize the importance of these selection aids in making acquisition decisions. These standard sources are consulted in the selection of core titles, but they are used differently than in the normal course of collection development. Although a positive review or a listing in an authoritative bibliography can provide sufficient justification for purchasing a title for the general collection, this is not the case in core selection. Additional information must be sought to determine that the title is truly exceptional and ultimately warrants core designation. For example, *Public Library Core Collection: Fiction* (formerly *Fiction Catalog*), *Public Library Core Collection: Nonfiction* (formerly *Public Library Catalog*), and reviews in *Choice* and *Library Journal*, all standard selection aids, are consulted, but each is just one step in a core selector's search to find the best titles from among the apparently limitless wealth of selection opportunities available.

Core selectors usually compare review media and "best of" lists after identifying a title as a potential core candidate. Selectors must approach every selection aid with a measure of cynicism, along with an understanding of the stated and unstated purposes of the source being consulted. This is crucial, because core selectors must utilize the most stringent of criteria whenever ascertaining the merits of a potential core title. This is the gist of the entire core process: determining which are the preeminent titles written for the educated layperson—difficult, yes, but not impossible.

Using selection aids properly is of the utmost importance in core decisions. When selecting a core title, it behooves us to do all the work necessary to search out the finest that has been written on any subject; it is far better to select fewer titles than inferior ones. In the case of some subject areas, such as medicine or computers, we must exercise great care to include only titles that are not time sensitive. For example, *Gray's Anatomy* or *A Child Is Born* by Lennart Nilsson would qualify as medical core titles. There are subject areas where there just are no truly excellent titles. A forum full of librarian cat lovers discovered, much to their dismay, that there was no single cat book similar to the American Kennel Club's *Complete Dog Book*, so none was designated core—a difficult omission, but an appropriate one. A core collection does not need to be well rounded. A core collection does not stand alone; there is an entire collection of noncore titles on the library shelves to supplement it. Remember: When in doubt, just leave it out!

As a designated core selector, you begin, individually or as a member of a core committee in larger library systems, to determine which selection resources have credibility for your library and will be used to ferret out your core titles. Deciding which selection aids to use can be difficult, for numerous resources are available. Typically certain titles are cited often in various national bibliographies. When you look up their reviews, you find them to be excellent. These same titles are often also prize winners and appear in "best of" lists. A pattern develops of what I call "hits," where the same title is recommended over and over again or deemed excellent in many of the standard selection aids. When this happens, you have discovered your first core title nomination.

The following discussion presents an overview of the basic types of selection aids that can prove useful in core list preparation. Selectors undoubtedly already use many of these selection tools in ongoing collection development work; however, in core work they are approached differently. Unfortunately, there are not just one or two sources that librarians can use and depend on always to yield core titles. In fact, there are numerous sources that can be consulted to unearth core selections. Librarians must know where to look for these selection aids and, most important, know how to use them correctly. To this end, I define the major types of selection aids and provide representative examples. I describe their individual points of view and explain their strengths and weaknesses. This is in no way an attempt to list all the possible sources for core selection but merely to provide an understanding of how these selection sources can best be used to determine core titles and point the way to a broader base of selection tools. Additional titles to assist you in further core selection work appear in the annotated source bibliography in chapter 6. Also, selection aids for specific subject core title selection accompany the sample core lists in chapter 7.

Book Reviews

Published book reviews are librarians' principal source for the majority of their book and media selections. For the purpose of this discussion, no distinction is made between printed reviews and those accessed online. In core selection, unlike most other selection, reviews are examined after a selector has compiled a list of core possibilities drawn from bibliographies, award winners, and best-book lists. This is possible because immediacy is not of primary importance in core collection development. After all, a core title should be timeless by its very definition. A core selector approaches reviews with preselected titles in the hope of validating a core possibility. These sources enable librarians to find out what experienced reviewers and subject experts have said about a proposed core title. Understanding the politics of reviewing is essential so that librarians, who are likely familiar with these review sources, can understand the partisanship that exists within the reviewing network. Selectors must be savvy about the entire review process to ensure that their core selection decisions are appropriate.

Reviews can be broken down into four distinct kinds on the basis of the audience for whom the review is being written: the general public, the specialist, the bookseller, the librarian. Most librarians rely on a few standard sources written either for the library profession or the book trade. The four most common are *Library Journal, Booklist, Kirkus Reviews,* and *Publishers Weekly.* Although each of these has a different editorial policy, they mostly review the same books with concise appraisals of the content.

Each of the four has different strengths and weaknesses depending on intended audience, source of reviews, and currency of titles: *Library Journal, Booklist,* and *Kirkus* are written specifically for librarians. They frequently discuss readership level, compare the title to others in the field, and make recommendations for purchase on the basis of library size and type. Most of their reviews, with the exception of those from *Kirkus* and special prepublication sections, tend to appear after a book's publication, limiting their usefulness as selection tools for new titles. However, this is irrelevant to core selection because a brand-new title is rarely designated as core. In most cases, enough time must elapse for a core possibility to be sufficiently reviewed and considered a possible candidate for yearly "best of" lists and inclusion in standard bibliographies. Reviews appearing in *Booklist, Publishers Weekly,* and *Kirkus* are written by the journals' staff members and by freelance contributors, all of whom have either library or publishing experience. Starred titles in *Kirkus* and other review media should be noted, for these are the very titles that in a year or two might be considered for core inclusion.

The librarian reviewers for *Library Journal,* though well meaning, are unpaid, and their evaluations can be uneven. Perhaps because librarians so value the written word and books in general, it is rare to find a negative review in this source. Inclusion in *Booklist* means that the title is recommended, which leaves one to wonder whether a title that is not reviewed was rejected or overlooked—something we will never know. Reviewers for library publications are quite good about comparing similar titles to the one that is currently being reviewed, a feature particularly useful when you are deciding which of the many titles on a topic warrant core consideration. Throughout the year, both *Library Journal* and *Booklist* publish what they term "core collection lists." Although these are far more extensive than our narrow definition of core titles here, they are excellent sources for core candidates. In anticipation of the 2009 bicentennial anniversaries of both Abraham Lincoln's and Charles Darwin's births, *Booklist,* for example, published recommended "core" titles on these men. Often such landmark celebrations result in a slew of books being published with perhaps a few worthy of inclusion in a core collection. The ensuing reviews often compare these new releases to existing titles, providing an excellent opportunity to examine and update your library's core collection in a particular subject area.

Publishers Weekly, written to alert booksellers to new titles, highlights books that will be heavily promoted and have sales potential. *Kirkus,* which also reviews books before their publication, is geared to librarians and is more concerned with the quality of a title than its marketability. Although this is extremely helpful in allowing librarians to order books in anticipation of demand by their library users, it has little significance for the selection of core titles. This is not to say that reviews written for the librarian or bookseller are not of help in the selection of core titles. When reading current book reviews, core selectors can look for potential core titles and make note of them. Certain key phrases signal a possible future core title: "best book on the subject," "landmark work," "despite the topic, a page turner from start to finish," "certain to be a prize winner." All these alert the core selector that this title bears consideration. Selectors should note such a highly touted title and follow the progress of its evaluation to see if it continues to impress reviewers. If it continues to receive widespread admiration, it is certain to appear in bibliographies and may ultimately win a major literary prize. These are the titles you want to watch and personally evaluate when they appear in your library or local bookstore.

In 2000, for example, North America's most famous birder, David Allen Sibley, who many consider the heir apparent to Roger Tory Peterson, teamed up with the National Audubon Society to publish *The Sibley Guide to Birds*. The book received consistently outstanding reviews, with even the venerable *New York Times* exclaiming that "once in a great while, a natural history book changes the way people look at the world."[11] *Time* magazine reviewed Sibley's guide when it was first released and then several months later did a follow-up article on its effect on the birding world and potentially on bird conservation. *Time* maintained that the guide was "the fastest-selling bird book in history" and was "attracting fresh recruits to birding all across America," even while "some 15 percent of the 800 species that live in or pass through North America are in serious decline." *Time* agreed with author Sibley that "the birds can still be saved, . . . if the millions of bird watchers band together to become a political force for conservation."[12] The tremendous acclaim and interest generated by *The Sibley Guide to Birds* surely make it an immediate core contender, perhaps even an "instant" classic—an oxymoron, perhaps, but one that underscores the instant recognition that can accompany a new book and immediately mark it as an important work.

Choice magazine, although geared to the academic librarian, can be a fine source for scholarly reviews for the public library selector. A quarter of the titles reviewed are from university presses, which are rarely reviewed elsewhere. *Choice* reviews are timeless and are written by university professors or teaching faculty who are subject specialists as well as academic librarians, many with advanced degrees. *Choice* reviewers all have a commitment to excellence in scholarship and often present the first "postpublication" peer evaluation of a scholarly title. Writers are knowledgeable and do a consistently fine job of comparing the presentation and importance of the title being reviewed to older literature in the field. The *Choice* yearly list of "Outstanding Academic Titles" is an excellent resource for core candidates.

In addition to reviews written specifically for the librarian or bookseller, there are many reviews written for the general public. The *New York Times Book Review*, the *New York Review of Books*, and *TLS* (formerly the *Times*

Literary Supplement) are the predominant ones devoted exclusively to book reviews. These reviews are almost always signed, and the wary selector should always pay attention to who is writing the review and where it is published.

Michael Korda, editor-in-chief of Simon and Schuster, has written about "the politics of book reviewing." He claims that

> the process by which book reviews are assigned carries with it an almost subliminal agenda on the part of the publication. They are often handed out to people whose opinions coincide with that of the editorial page of the newspaper or who are well known to the book-review editor so that it's easy enough to guess what they'll write. Books with ideas that are "unpopular," or are deemed to be "reactionary," are often given to people who are reasonably certain to attack and belittle those ideas.

Korda relates that, when Simon and Schuster published Ronald Reagan's autobiography in 1990, "it was amazing how many newspapers sent it out for review to people whose politics were the opposite of Reagan's." Korda experienced the same situation with his own book. Richard Nixon, whose books Korda had edited, wrote "Join the club! As I read the sh-tty review of your book I realized again that when the editors of [a major book review] don't like the thesis of a book—fiction or nonfiction—they pick a reviewer who shares their prejudice."[13]

A selector should always consider the potential "politics" surrounding a book review. There might be personal pettiness on the part of the reviewer. For example, note who has written a front-page review for the *New York Times Book Review*. Is the reviewer another novelist? Someone concerned about receiving a negative review in retaliation? Has this writer-turned-reviewer recently lost a prestigious award to the very author whose work is being reviewed? James Altas, in his article "Books: Everyone's a Critic," discusses our country's top novelists who write book reviews, often for the *Times*, and their personal inclinations. For example, he notes that both Joyce Carol Oates and John Irving (two award-winning core authors) never review books they do not like as a matter of principle. Oates reports that she will not "review a book that I don't have anything good to say about. . . . I write to recommend books." Irving said he reviewed only books he liked because "I won't wreck my voice with that bitchy tone we employ when something doesn't wholly please us."[14] Who is writing a review and where it is published, whether it be in the *New York Times Book Review* or *Library Journal*, provide valuable insight into the reviewers' personal biases and help you delve beyond the review's actual text to determine a book's merit.

To help you get started in evaluating reviews, you might want to take a look at the *Books of the Century*, an excellent compilation of original book reviews from the *New York Times Book Review* of outstanding books of the twentieth century, quite a few of which were not initially reviewed positively. The more reviews you read, the better able you are to uncover a reviewer's or editor's personal agenda. Over time, you will begin to identify those reviewers and magazines whose opinions you can trust. At the same time, though, always keep an open mind when reading reviews, and be wary not to let your personal opinions sway you one way or the other—another reason it is extremely important that you keep searching for positive and diversified "hits" for all potential core titles. The *New York Times Book Review* also publishes a yearly "10 Best Books of the Year," which always has strong possibilities for core collections.

Keep track of the upcoming titles with reviews that piqued your interest, and make a point of examining them when they arrive in your library to determine if you agree with the reviewer's assessment. This might seem like an inordinate amount of work, but most of us who are always on the lookout for good books to read do this to a lesser degree anyway. You will just be taking this one step farther by seeing if you agree with a reviewer's judgment. Over time, you will begin to see patterns in reviews and magazines and will be better able to determine which of these best serve your core development needs. Building a foundation of knowledge greatly enhances your ability to base selection decisions on reviews. Understanding the focus of particular review media, their intended audience, and the ultimate purpose of their reviews will all prove valuable.

Countless other magazines regularly contain excellent general reviews—the *New Yorker, Harper's, Atlantic Monthly, Smithsonian,* and *Vanity Fair* to name but a few. Many regional newspapers print reviews and may have a special page or two devoted to books, which often are of local interest. The national *USA Today,* for example, has a special book section in its Thursday issue, complete with its weekly best-seller list and several reviews; some of these are wire service reprints from other national newspapers, but many are written especially for *USA Today.* Weekly news magazines, like *Time* and *Newsweek,* regularly contain book reviews. The *New York Times Book Review,* the *New York Review of Books,* and *TLS* are exclusively reviews; all the others include reviews only as one of their many features. Titles reviewed in most are selected on the basis of what editors think will be of interest to their particular readership and are likely to be positive. Less-than-positive reviews are common in both the *New Yorker* and *Harper's,* which bemoan the state of publishing and books in this day and age—a familiar theme with these two literary magazines.

A staggering number of topical reviews are written for the general public. Just about every subject has its own specialty magazine, which usually includes relevant reviews. *Car and Driver, American History, Travel and Leisure, Psychology Today, Rolling Stone, Kiplinger's Personal Finance, Golf Digest,* and *PC World* are just a few; the list is endless. Although these journals are written for the general public, they assume some subject knowledge and interest on the part of their readership. These reviews can be a source of potential core titles, but it must be stressed that these sporadic reviews are not a comprehensive overview of books on a topic. Still, a core selector can assume that a title of importance on a particular subject will be reviewed at some point in a magazine strictly devoted to that subject, whether it be golf or finance. The librarian can be fairly certain that this reviewer has expertise on the book's subject, because this is essential to maintain the magazine's credibility with its knowledgeable subscribers.

One basic assumption of a book review is that it be free of any motive other than to inform the reader about the merits of a particular book. A reviewer should never be writing a review to gain approval of an author, to advance a personal political or religious interest, or as an advertising endorsement. Unfortunately, all this does occur. It behooves the librarian to pay attention to who is writing a review and to the editorial policies of the magazine in which the review appears. For example, Tiger Woods reviewing a book for *Golf Digest* and saying that it is the best book ever written on the golf swing might reasonably be thought to be a reliable endorsement of the book's merit—unless he is writing as part of a contractual endorsement or stresses the importance of a particular brand of golf clubs or shoes in his review. A magazine's editorial policy should clearly state its biases and the obligations of its reviewers. Many magazines include in the front of each issue a brief statement of their focus along with any political or commercial affiliation. A quick look at the opening editorial and the table of contents can assist a librarian in determining the validity of a journal's reviews.

Several bibliographies, such as *Ulrich's Periodicals Directory*, list complete information on magazines. Ulrich's multivolume set is arranged by subject and contains over 225,000 periodicals, including serials only available online. Ulrichsweb, Ulrich's online subscription, contains even more periodicals. Both supply complete bibliographic and descriptive information for each entry along with any appropriate URLs, e-mail addresses, or websites (see the periodical guides in chapter 6 for additional information). Familiarity with a magazine's policy and its reviewers helps enormously in your ability to assess a reviewed title's worth to your library.

ForeWord Magazine, known for its esteemed reviews of titles from small publishers, has launched ForeWordreviews.com, where anyone can get a book reviewed for a relatively nominal fee. This is a logical step to assist self-published online authors as well as small-press writers get their work reviewed. *ForeWord's* publisher explains that "there are a lot of great books coming to independent presses that don't have a voice to get noticed." Further, "why do publishers and authors have to depend on a select group of New York review publications to determine whether their book is good or bad?"[15] Nonetheless, there is certainly a conflict of interest in having a customer or publisher pay the reviewer's salary. This demonstrates again why it is vital that librarians know as much as possible about review sources and reviewers, so as to make informed core selection decisions.

In addition to reviews written for the general public, the librarian, and the bookseller, other reviews are written specifically for and by the subject specialist. Because the main purpose of a core title is to stretch readers' minds and expand their knowledge, a scholarly or technical title may be appropriate as a core title. Reviews written for "the doctor, the lawyer, and the candlestick maker" can be useful for core selection as long as the book has sufficient readability to interest the educated layperson. A physical inspection of a potential core title can be of particular value for books that have had only an academic or subject-specialist review, no matter how glowingly that reviewer wrote about the title. A specialist may see wonderful research or an unusual approach to a subject of great personal interest, enabling him or her to perhaps overlook pedantic or plodding writing. To appeal to the general public, a core title must be well written and accurate but still lively enough to hold readers' interest.

By no means am I saying that every academic title will always be too dull for the nonspecialist or that you should not consider technical books for your collection, just that any one of them may not be an appropriate core title selection. A true core title should grab the reader's attention, whatever the subject. One of the underlying principles of core selection is that a fine writer can make any subject interesting. As a core selector, you are searching for that special writer who can take a seemingly complex subject, inject her or his enthusiasm and knowledge, and write so well that it generates interest in your readers. Difficult to find, certainly; extraordinary, most definitely—core books by definition are extraordinary. Nonfiction writers with this special gift include Rachel Carson, writing about the dangers of pesticides in *Silent Spring*; Art Spiegelman, writing about and illustrating the unlikely topic of the Holocaust in his *Maus: A Survivor's Tale*, the first graphic novel to win a Pulitzer Prize; George Schaller, writing on animal research in *The Last Panda*; and Susan Orlean, writing about the orchid trade in *The Orchid Thief*. Remember, you are not looking for a certain number of books, only the very best books, the ones with literary merit, richness, and originality but with wide general appeal. Keep in mind the mantra of core collection development: When in doubt, just leave it out!

You may want to include a title that was published a while ago and may need to find review information to support your contention. Be aware that there are indexes to reviews. Some, like *Book Review Digest*, include review excerpts that can help you find information on previously published books. In addition, there are standard periodical guides, such as the *New York Times Index* and the *Readers' Guide to Periodical Literature*, which list reviews that have been published in magazines and newspapers. Online subscription databases, such as InfoTrac, ProQuest, or WilsonSelectPlus, often provide full text of reviews and are easy to use. Books in Print with Book Reviews is available as a two-disc subscription, which is updated monthly and includes full-text reviews from many of the standard selection sources, such as *Publishers Weekly, Choice, Booklist, Sci-Tech News*, and *Kirkus Reviews*. Additionally, Books in Print and Forthcoming Books are both available as Internet subscriptions (see www .booksinprint.com). These BIP products, along with Title Source III, which is library vendor Baker and Taylor's online title-information database; or ipage, which is jobber Ingram's, can all be used to track an author or title along with its reviews. Amazon is an excellent source for reviews; it lists most titles with a wide range of previously published reviews, along with individual customer reviews, which can give you an inkling of the readability and general appeal of a title. Bookseller Barnes and Noble's website (www.barnesandnoble.com) provides descriptive summaries of newer titles as well as reviews. Arts and Letters Daily (www.aldaily.com) is an excellent website that provides links to many of the major book review sources, along with links to dozens of newspapers and news services. These sites can help you ascertain whether a title warrants inclusion in a core collection. Additionally, there are numerous multivolume sets of criticism and biography that can be consulted to determine the importance of authors or their writings (see chapter 6).

Advertisements and Publishers' Catalogs

As we are all too well aware, advertising surrounds us. Many of the magazines discussed earlier have advertisements touting recently published books. Titles that appear in ads are often endorsed by famous and best-selling authors. Writers, as part of their publishing contracts, must countenance a certain number of books and frequently have no say in which titles they must support. Ads might include excerpts from published reviews. Be aware that these are often snippets of a longer review that may have been taken out of context and may not be accurate. Savvy reviewers try to write their reviews in a manner that makes this eventuality less likely.

Sony's Columbia Pictures, for example, was recently caught creating a fake critic to praise one of its newly released movies. Other Hollywood studios also admitted to this practice and to using actors and employees in testimonial ads. Studios have been known to pay critics to fly to New York City or Los Angeles, where they put them up in fancy hotels and give them access to movie stars. Lesser-known critics often feel obligated to praise the film or risk being taken off the "junket list." Peter Rainer, the chair of the National Society of Film Critics, said that "such 'blurbmeisters' have been a problem for a long time. . . . He claims that his society considered lobbying the studios to stop using people who are 'an extension of advertising publicity departments.'"[16] On the whole, studios prefer to use quotes from well-known critics, but when necessary they use quotes from little-known publications. A USA Today study of movie review quotations found that "in most cases, review snippets that were used came from well-known critics and publications."[17] Still, it is worth looking at advertisements to see what publishers and film studios are marketing and what is believed to be the important selling point of a particular book or film. Who is quoted in an ad and what they say or do not say can tell you a lot. An interesting promotional blurb may entice you to find out more about a particular title; on the other hand, a blurb that says nothing alluring can also tell you something about the book or film.

Librarians are inundated with publishers' catalogs, flyers, along with online newsletters and can use these as good sources for potential selection information. Because the purpose of a publisher's catalog or website is to sell books, its contents must be evaluated with that in mind. Experienced selectors, although aware that these are nothing more than sales promotions, know enough about individual publishers' and authors' strengths and weaknesses to be able to form a preliminary opinion on the advertised titles. Both professions desire the same thing—readers for their books. Many times, catalogs, like advertisements, are the first inkling a librarian has that a book is to be released. Publishers' catalogs, whether online or in print, are excellent barometers of public interest and can be of tremendous assistance when speed is crucial in meeting library demand. Spending some time looking beyond the basic information in a catalog can enable a selector to determine the importance a publisher is placing on a new book. How much actual catalog space is given to one title? Has an older title been reissued in a spiffy new edition or perhaps as a special edition with a reader's guide and author interview bound right into the book? This special reprint edition shows that a publisher feels the title has staying power and is willing to take a chance on republishing it. Any awards that a title received are almost always listed in a publisher's catalog or website as well.

Publishers and vendors often provide lists of what they consider standard library titles. Although these are in truth more like add and replacement lists, they are definitely worth checking to see if you have overlooked any potential core titles. Many vendors have opening-day collection lists that can also prove helpful. The advantage of these checklists is that the titles listed are currently in print and therefore easily available for purchase. Publishers such as Random House, which has classic imprints such as Vintage Classics and the Modern Library series, are excellent sources for core titles. Random House's yearly publication "Freshman Year Reading" is a descriptive and well-annotated list of titles recommended by its academic department as being of particular significance for incoming college students, many of which are core titles. Just remember, whenever you use a publisher's catalog as a checklist, this is only one publisher with the goal of selling you its books; there are undoubtedly important works from other publishers that will not be listed.

Larger libraries and even smaller ones also receive regular calls and visits from publisher and sales representatives. These advertising plugs can be misleading and are of limited value in core selection. If you think a book has potential for your library, do not hesitate to ask a sales rep or the publisher directly for a free review copy. Be certain to explain that you are considering the title for your core collection, which may result in a substantial order at a later date. Smaller libraries can ask for an approval copy, which they are able to return at no charge if the title is not selected for their library. A library is under no obligation to return or purchase an unsolicited book.

Publishers may ask if you would like to receive review copies on an ongoing basis. Jobbers such as Baker and Taylor and Ingram also have advance-look programs and regularly send reading copies from uncorrected proofs to their library customers. If you decide to participate in these programs, be forewarned that a reading copy is not a final edition; major changes may still be made or the book publication delayed. Reading copies are not to be added to your library's collection and are not to be sold, even at Friends of the Library book sales or to used-book stores. You must discard them after reading and making a selection decision.

Examination of reading copies can assist librarians in making selection decisions; however, keep in mind that the distribution and printing of reading copies are part of a publisher's or distributor's marketing plan. Publishers and jobbers may ask if you are willing to write an endorsement for one of their titles. Sometimes this can result in your library receiving gift books, or it can be a requirement for your continuing to receive advance reading copies. Librarians should check with their supervisors about a library's policy on endorsements before agreeing to do this. Make certain that whatever you write is truthful and something you would not object to seeing in a future advertisement or publisher's catalog with your name or your library's name attached to it.

Advertising is endemic to the publishing industry, although at times this is not directly apparent and can lead to an erroneous selection decision. Besides paying for the obvious magazine advertisements, reading copies, and splashy catalogs, publishers also pay to have their books displayed prominently in the front of stores or in cardboard "dumps." They may have paid to have their titles included in a bookstore's special newsletters and can pay as much as $10,000 to have their books recommended electronically in online bookstore Amazon's e-mail to its customers.[18] Selectors must consistently question whether a title is recommended because of its intrinsic merit or merely as part of a publishing promotion.

Bibliographies as Checklists

Bibliographies of recommended books can be useful guides for librarians determining the "best books." These retrospective checklists are most often used to verify a library's holdings to ascertain what needs to be added to a collection, to evaluate a collection by determining what proportion of a recommended bibliography a library contains, or to assist in making deselection decisions. In the case of core selection, bibliographies are used primarily as checklists to see whether a certain book is a core candidate. They are part of the ongoing quest to secure another vote of confidence for a specific core title—to provide yet one more positive "hit" for a particular book. Like any of the other selection sources already discussed, these bibliographies are only aids to core selection. None of them can ever be the definitive word on what should be designated core for your individual library. Before using a particular bibliography to establish a title's merits, it is important that you review it first, using much the same criteria you would use in evaluating any reference tool. A good place to begin is to read the bibliography's introduction, which establishes the criteria and parameters of a specific checklist.

In *Collection Development*, Katz lists seven criteria to consider when determining the worth of a bibliography as a potential selection aid. These cover the basics and all are of importance in evaluating a bibliography's worth for core collection development:

1 | *Scope.* How much is included and in what subjects?

2 | *Audience.* For whom is this intended?

3 | *Annotations.* Are there any? Are they critical or merely descriptive?

4 | *Timeliness.* Are the titles still in print and available? What time period is covered? How current are included titles?

5 | *Selection.* How were the titles selected? By committee? Is the publisher reputable?

6 | *Recommendations.* Are there any? Is every title included recommended?

7 | *Format.* Is it easy to use? Full and correct bibliographic information included? Adequate indexes?[19]

Once you locate a bibliography that appears to be an appropriate source, you can begin using it to locate potential core titles. As you create your core title list, it is a good idea to make note of any reviews or bibliographies you used to select individual core titles. This method enables you to see a "hit" pattern emerging as a certain title is consistently rated highly in checklist after checklist. Keeping track of these "hits" serves as an excellent point of reference to remind you why you decided to designate a particular title as core. It also proves extremely helpful if you ever have to defend your core choices to your colleagues, and it assists other selectors who may be assigned to review your core selections. Keep track of this information on index cards or with database software. If a book selection work form already exists, perhaps you can adapt it; if not, a specific core work form could be created. However you decide to proceed, I would suggest some uniformity in recording core candidate data. An outline in chapter 5 shows the information a core work form should contain.

There are several standard bibliographies that you should consult regularly when compiling a core list. The two bibliographies most commonly used by selectors in public libraries are published by the H. W. Wilson Company, which has recently changed both of these titles: *Fiction Catalog* and *Public Library Catalog* became *Public Library Core Collection: Fiction* and *Public Library Core Collection: Nonfiction*. Needless to say, even though these sources are now termed "core collections," their thousands of titles are well beyond the scope of the outstanding core collection that we are talking about developing in this book. Despite their new nomenclature, the focus of these catalogs remains essentially unchanged. It is interesting that in the ten years since the first edition of these collections, the term *core collection* has become a catch phrase, used frequently, as we have seen, by library publications, vendors, and publishers. This can be confusing, so be aware that this is the case and always remember how specific and circumscribed our definition remains. The *Public Library Core Collection: Fiction* and *Public Library Core Collection: Nonfiction* print editions are updated with yearly supplements. A fully revised bound edition of each is released every four or five years, and the online editions are updated quarterly. The eight thousand plus titles in the *Public Library Core Collection: Fiction* are selected on the basis of staff recommendations from an advisory committee of librarians across the country and, according to the H. W. Wilson website, cover "the best authors and their widely read works in literary and popular fiction, old and new." Collections, out-of-print titles, and large-type titles are also included. Full bibliographic information and excerpts from reviews are given for every title. The bibliography is arranged by author. A valuable title and subject index is included along with a directory of publishers whose books are listed in the catalog.

The companion *Public Library Core Collection: Nonfiction* follows the same basic Wilson format and includes over nine thousand nonfiction titles all recommended for public libraries. Titles are briefly annotated and arranged in volumes by subject. These bibliographies of recommended titles for public libraries likely contain most of your core books among the many thousands of titles listed. The difficulty comes with deciding which are truly core titles.

In addition to these general checklists, there are many subject bibliographies for you to consult when compiling subject core lists. Chapter 6 includes some of the most helpful of these along with a brief description of their contents. In chapter 7 examples of subject bibliographies can be found.

Award Winners and Best-Books Lists

Prestigious book awards are an excellent source of core titles. Although occasionally the politics of selecting boards and their awards have been questioned, every National Book Award winner and each Pulitzer and Nobel Prize winner must be viewed as a likely core title. These are the three most important literary awards given every year. A few of these award-winning titles or authors may not have appeal for a particular library's community, but as a general rule these books can be considered to have the highest literary quality. The publicity and hubbub that surround these books often create community interest. Although winning one of these preeminent awards does not guarantee the same commercial success as being awarded the comparable Caldecott Medal for excellence in children's literature, no library can go wrong in purchasing these prize winners. In addition, it is an excellent idea for core selectors to read every year's National Book Award and each Pulitzer Prize winner in order to establish a mental benchmark of what exactly is the best writing. Whether you agree with every prize selection or not, this firsthand knowledge helps enormously as you continuously examine titles for core collection inclusion.

The Pulitzer Prize is named in honor of the Hungarian-born U.S. newspaper publisher Joseph Pulitzer, whose journalistic format set the style for the modern newspaper. After his death in 1911, funds provided in his will established the Columbia University School of Journalism and the annual Pulitzer prizes. Yearly prizes are given for the best books in the categories of fiction, nonfiction, poetry, biography, drama, and history. The National Book Awards, selected by members of the National Book Foundation, are handed out to the best fiction, nonfiction, and poetry titles of the past year.

The annual Nobel Prize is an international prize, first awarded in 1901 under the will of the Swedish chemist Alfred Nobel. Prizes are given to the persons who have made the greatest contribution in the fields of physics, chemistry, medicine, world peace, and literature. The Nobel Prize in literature is awarded not for a single book but for an author's entire body of work. Authors who win this prize should have all their writings reviewed, and a representative title should be considered for inclusion in the library's core collection.

In 2008 the final Book Sense Book of the Year Award, formerly called the ABBY, was awarded. The Book Sense was created by the ABA in 1991 to honor those literary "treasures" that ABA bookstore members most enjoyed recommending to their customers during the previous year. In 2009 the ABA changed the award to the Indies Choice Book Awards and invited their customers to help select the winners. There are now three adult selections: Best Indie Buzz Book (fiction), Best Conversation Starter (nonfiction), and Best Author Discovery. Although it remains to be seen how helpful these new awards will be in selecting core titles, I would recommend looking at them. The United Kingdom's Mann Booker and Costa Book (formerly Whitbread) award winners and semifinalists should also be considered to have core potential. Both awards, established about thirty years ago to acknowledge fine writers and to raise public awareness of high-quality literature, are now the most prestigious literary awards given in Great Britain and Ireland. There are countless literary prizes awarded every year that can also be consulted; several are listed in chapter 6. When you are selecting any award winner for the core collection, remember to note which prize the title received.

If you are just beginning to establish a core collection, consider the entire backlist of award winners from a prize's inception to the current year. Undoubtedly a few titles have become dated and no longer need to be included in your core collection. Yet many of these previous award recipients still have validity for today's readers. Looking at the runner-up titles for a particular award, if they are revealed, can prove fruitful as well.

Each year since 1944, an ALA committee has selected and published a list of "Notable Books." These are fiction and nonfiction titles selected for their literary merit and readability. The purpose of the list is to call attention to these significant titles and encourage people to read them. In the 1990s, the ALA established a publicity subcommittee to increase the visibility and prestige of the list by having publishers include the Notable Book designation in press releases, advertisements, book blurbs, and on the books themselves with seals. This is an excellent source created specifically for public libraries and should be examined yearly for potential core titles. The ALA's list of "Outstanding Books for the College Bound" is another publication worth reviewing. Both lists are also published on the association's website, www.ala.org.

Many of the awards discussed here, such as the Nobel and Pulitzer, also have their own websites. A complete list of the major prize winners can be found in the World Almanac (www.worldalmanac.com) and on the ABA website (www.bookweb.org). The *New York Times Book Review* also publishes an Editor's Choice list of the year's outstanding books. *Library Journal* and *Booklist* do as well, along with lists of the best titles in specific subject areas, compiled by specialists.

Perhaps spearheaded by Oprah's Book Club, there has recently been an explosion in the number of reading clubs. When Oprah Winfrey began a book club on her television talk show, she sent bookstores and libraries scrambling to fill requests for the titles she recommended as these books roared onto the national best-seller lists. Her choices are mostly general popular fiction; all continue to be easy to read and emotionally engaging for her legions of female fans. Some of her choices were award winners and of more universal appeal, like Toni Morrison's *Song of Solomon*, Ernest Gaines's *A Lesson before Dying*, and Barbara Kingsolver's *Poisonwood Bible*. A complete list of her selections appears on her website (www.oprah.com), which is worth reviewing for potential core titles.

Thanks in part to Oprah using her personality and popularity to tout books and reading groups, there are now several books that offer assistance in setting up reading groups. Many of these handbooks contain fine reading lists compiled and used by book clubs across the nation. *The Reading Group Book* by David Laskin and Holly Hughes includes annotated lists of more than 250 titles arranged by categories. *The Readers' Choice* by Victoria Golden McMains supplies 200 book club favorites with page-long descriptions that the author collected from more than seventy reading groups nationwide. *The Reading Group Handbook* by Rachel W. Jacobsohn, herself a professional reading group leader, supplies over thirty-five suggested reading lists. These lists are all worth examining because they provide yet another opportunity to test the worthiness of a core candidate. Publishers' and book suppliers' websites, such as Amazon or Barnes and Noble, also list book club suggestions along with reading group guides; additional book-related websites are listed in chapter 6.

No matter what you think of Oprah and all the hype surrounding her book club picks, she has single-handedly lifted what publishers term the "midlist book" onto the best-seller lists. These midlist titles are thoughtful and artfully written books by lesser-known authors that as a rule do not sell as well as the formula best-sellers of John Sandford, James Patterson, or Stephenie Meyer. The well-crafted book that appears on the best-seller list is truly something special. *Cold Mountain* by Charles Frazier, *Snow Falling on Cedars* by David Guterson, and the Pulitzer Prize–winning *Beloved* by Toni Morrison were all midlist titles that became best-sellers. All combine exquisite writing, unforgettable characters, and storytelling with great readability. Astoundingly, they all appeared for many, many weeks on nationwide best-seller lists, refuting librarians who dispute the potential value of any and all best-sellers. Bearing possible exceptions in mind, it is important that core selectors regularly look at the major best-seller lists, such as those from the *New York Times* and *USA Today*, which can contain core possibilities that have a proven track record of widespread popular appeal. These extraordinary books combine the best of both worlds—best-sellers, yet they fit this guide's definition of *core:* of the highest quality, class, and rank.

In addition to the best-seller and "best of" lists, there are numerous other basic lists developed specifically for librarians. *Good Reading: A Guide for Serious Readers*, published by R. R. Bowker, annotates almost three thousand titles and is one such source. Bowker's *Best Books for Public Libraries* is another annotated list of the "top" ten thousand fiction and nonfiction titles. The *Reader's Catalog* from the *New York Review of Books*, which is also annotated, lists over forty thousand titles that the editors term "the most interesting and informative books in print today . . . a 'Dream Library.'" Libraries Unlimited's *Genreflecting* is a fun guide to genre fiction and an extremely helpful source for readers' advisory work as well as suggestions for genre core titles.

Many books written for the general public can provide core candidates. These are inherently a celebration of books, often accompanied by well-thought-out reading lists. Ronald B. Shwartz's *For the Love of Books* is such a title. It shares the favorite books of major contemporary writers, such as Robert Bly, Rita Mae Brown, and Michael Ondaatje. *Great Books for Every Book Lover*, compiled by Thomas Craughwell, offers personal recommendations on a wide range of subjects arranged in intriguing and amusing chapters: "A Masterpiece You Might Have Missed," "Great Adventures," "Great Gossip," "An Author You Should Know." E. D. Hirsch's *Cultural Literacy* (the intriguing and controversial lists were discussed in chapter 1) is another possible provider of core titles, along with the 89 Great Books of the Western World chosen by Mortimer Adler listed in Alex Beam's *A Great Idea at the Time. 1001 Books You Must Read before You Die* is a "bucket list" of titles selected by literary critics that they felt made "an impact—whether in the form of critical acclaim or cult classic." Nancy Pearl's *Book Lust* and *More Book Lust* are fun guides to books the former Seattle librarian recommends "for every mood, moment, and reason." Admittedly not all these books with book lists are as helpful as others, but they should alert you to the infinite variety of basic book lists that are available to assist you in your quest for the best core titles. Remember to always make certain to note the source of recommendations for a potential core title. Doing this immediately saves you a lot of searching later on in the core process and adds credibility to your core recommendations. See chapter 6 for additional basic list suggestions.

PERSONAL EXAMINATION OF CORE CANDIDATES

After you have read all the glowing reviews of a potential core title and seen it listed repeatedly in various book lists (or perhaps it has just won the National Book Award), it is crucial that you personally examine the book. I cannot stress enough how important it is that you look at every single core possibility. Often these titles are already in your library; rarely are they brand-new titles. If your library does not have the title and the budget permits, you might order the title for your general collection and make a note to review it when it arrives. If your budget cannot justify this expense, you can try requesting a review copy from the publisher. If this fails, order a copy through interlibrary loan or locate it at a local college or university library. You might even try to examine it on your next visit to your favorite bookstore.

What are you looking for in a potential core title? Basically you are looking for "curb" appeal. The book should be user-friendly. How does this book look? Is it an attractive edition and well bound? David Ebershoff, publishing director of the Modern Library editions, explains the continued success of this imprint which, although founded in 1917, continues to publish "tried and true classics," with over three hundred titles in print. According to Ebershoff, the packaging of Modern Library books has become "hipper and less academic." The book cover art might feature a scene from a newly released film based on the title, thus creating renewed interest in a classic. He mentions that Isak Dinesen's *Out of Africa* was not particularly popular until the 1985 film starring Meryl Streep came out, and now years later Dinesen is still selling.[20]

As you examine core classics, you begin to recognize editions that offer good value along with attractive packaging and durability. Often classic and core titles exist in numerous different editions and printings. You want to order the one that is most likely to engage your clientele's interest. Commemorative or anniversary editions of classics frequently have forewords written by another writer in the field that can help illuminate the subject or explain the historical significance of the title. For example, Diane Johnson, the author of the best-selling *Le Divorce*, wrote the introduction to Modern Library's *Jane Eyre*, and Kathryn Harrison, author of the erotic novel *The Kiss*, wrote the introduction to Nathaniel Hawthorne's *Scarlet Letter*. On occasion the original author might also write a special essay or revise the work to add meaning for today's reader and renew interest in reading a classic or core title. These editions can be quite attractive, and the additional information can enhance the reader's enjoyment.

There are many editions of Shakespeare's *Hamlet*, and you need to decide if one edition is superior in appearance and value. Certainly the movie tie-in edition with Mel Gibson on the cover makes that edition more appealing to some of today's library users. Does one edition have better explanatory notes or are the footnotes clearer, making it more accessible to the layperson? If you find one edition to be better than the others, you must then decide whether to require every agency to have this particular version of *Hamlet* instead of the others they might already own. You may choose to suggest that this edition be purchased only whenever *Hamlet* needs to be replaced. Perhaps it could be a required purchase only for those agencies that have the most interested users along with sufficient dollars to spend on yet another edition of this play. In making these types of recommendations, you will always be more comfortable if you have personally viewed the book and can justify one edition over another.

Translations of the same title can vary greatly and have a huge impact on the readability and enjoyment of a classic. The best-selling, award-winning translator Richard Pevear discusses the difficulty of this task in the introduction to his and his wife's highly acclaimed translation of *War and Peace*: "It is often said that a good translation is one that 'does not feel like a translation,' one that reads 'smoothly' in 'idiomatic' English. But who determines the standard of the idiomatic. . . . Is Melville idiomatic? Is Faulkner?" Pevear maintains that a classic must reflect the time in which it was written: "It occurs in the space between two languages, and most often between two historical moments."[21] When different translations of a core title are available, it can prove difficult to decide which one to select. Online resources like Amazon or Google can allow you to actually compare the same paragraph in several editions. Most important is that the translation retain the spirit of the original without being either too old-fashioned for today's reader or inappropriately contemporary.

On occasion you may need to decide between two books on the same subject. A hands-on look at these books could be the deciding factor in designating one as core and the other not. There is no substitute for looking at the prints in an art book or the illustrations in a bird-watching title. For example, although you find that the prints in one van Gogh book are finer than those in another, you might decide that, even with better reproductions, you still cannot justify spending twice the money. If your core process involves committee meetings and forums, it is a good idea to take these different editions with you to show your colleagues and to help explain your decisions. You should always make notes on your observations to assist you in making your final recommendations and to help selectors who may be working with your core list at a later date.

In *How to Read a Book*, authors Mortimer Adler and Charles Van Doren call this cursory review "systematic skimming or pre-reading." The following are some of their suggestions on how to proceed to get the most "kernels of nourishment" from this "inspectional reading":

1 | Look at the title page and, if the book has one, at its preface.

2 | Study the table of contents to obtain a general sense of the book's structure; use it as a road map before taking a trip.

3 | Check the index. . . . Make a quick estimate of the range of topics covered and the kinds of books and authors referred to.

4 | Read the publisher's blurb.

5 | Look now at the chapters that seem to be pivotal to its argument.

6 | Finally, turn the pages, dipping in here and there, reading a paragraph or two, sometimes several pages in sequence, never more than that.

The authors maintain that if you follow this basic outline you will have now "skimmed the book systematically" and should know "a great deal about the book at this point after having spent no more than a few minutes, or at most an hour, with it." It is worth taking the time to complete a "systematic skimming" of every potential core title because core acceptance ultimately mandates that the title be added to every branch and the central library, a major expense for any library system.[22]

When examining a potential core title, you are evaluating the book according to standard criteria for general selection. These guidelines cover format (which includes durability, attractiveness, and value); appropriate intended audience (the educated layperson); a subject of interest to the community; comparison to similar works on the same subject; and overall readability. This last factor can best be determined by actually reading a chapter or two yourself. A true core title should immediately engage your interest while illuminating its subject. Again let me remind you: if you have any doubts about a core candidate's suitability, just leave it out. Not selecting a title as core does not preclude it being in your library; it is just not designated as core.

COMMUNITY INVOLVEMENT IN CORE SELECTION

There are times when all the selection aids discussed in this chapter do not seem sufficient. Occasionally, the more you research a title, the more confused you become about its suitability for core. This may be the ideal time to contact local community subject specialists for help. The core selectors of the Phoenix Public Library were encouraged to ask experts in the community for their core suggestions. On all occasions, these experts were flattered to be asked, knowledgeable, and impressed with our librarians' determination to find the best books for the citizens of Phoenix. Some of us thought that this interaction even helped us secure votes when library bonds were up for a general election.

Phoenix's unusually dry climate makes it difficult to find relevant gardening books that are reviewed or written specifically for the desert environment. Phoenix is home to the Desert Botanical Garden, one of the finest cactus gardens in the world, and the Garden's resident experts were very willing to suggest core titles and to review our core selections. We also contacted the Phoenix chapter of the Rose Society to see which books they found most useful for growing roses in the desert.

Our librarians spoke to their doctors, their car service managers, their tax accountants, their clergy, members of the local historical society—anyone who they felt had expertise beyond their own. The information gleaned was added to what selectors had discovered on their own. Selectors were always careful to remember that they were picking titles for the general public, the readers who possess a layperson's knowledge of a wide variety of subjects—not the subject specialist.

Core selectors also contacted their colleagues in the local college and university libraries along with professors teaching in subject areas. This proved particularly helpful where subject lists and review media were not as readily available. These consultants were invited to attend core forums. They were delighted to be asked, made a point of attending, and enjoyed answering staff members' questions about particular titles. They often recommended other colleagues who they felt would be helpful to the core process and would enjoy the experience. Beyond the core help that the library received, we made valuable contacts for program speakers and, on occasion, even received copies of core titles and special funding to purchase core titles within subject parameters.

SUMMARY

Determining which titles to include in a core collection is an elaborate and complicated process. Adler and Van Doren, in their classic guide to reading, *How to Read a Book*, discuss how to learn "to pigeonhole a book." The authors outline four basic questions that must be asked when evaluating any book:

1 | What is the book about as a whole? You must try to discover the leading theme of the book, and how the author develops the theme in an orderly way by subdividing it into its essential subordinate themes or topics.

2 | What is being said in detail, and how? You must try to discover the main ideas, assertions, and arguments that constitute the author's particular message.

3 | Is the book true, in whole or part? You cannot answer this question until you have answered the first two. You have to know what is being said before you can decide whether it is true or not. . . . You

are obligated . . . to make up your own mind. Knowing the author's mind is not enough.

4 | What of it? If the book has given you information, you must ask about its significance. Why does the author think it is important to know these things? Is it important to you to know them?[23]

Core selectors need to ask themselves these four questions whenever they review any of the selection aids outlined in this chapter or personally examine a potential core title. This is certainly not an easy task; it is one that uses all of a librarian's extensive knowledge and experience. There is no doubt that core selection can prove intimidating, because we all have different educational backgrounds, reading habits, and areas of subject expertise. Developing a core collection is truly a graduate seminar for librarians; it expands selectors' familiarity with books and keeps them current on the best of what is available and being written today. Enjoy the time spent on core collection development; it is truly the "browser's ecstasy."

Notes

1. G. Edward Evans, *Developing Library and Information Center Collections*, 2nd ed. (Littleton, Colo.: Libraries Unlimited, 1987), 21.
2. Haines quoted in ibid., 91.
3. Victoria Golden McMains, *The Readers' Choice: 200 Book Club Favorites* (New York: HarperCollins, 2000), 2.
4. William A. Katz, *Collection Development: The Selection of Materials for Libraries* (New York: Holt, 1980), 89.
5. Ibid.
6. Daniel T. Richards, "By Your Selection Criteria Are Ye Known," *Library Acquisitions: Practice and Theory* 15 (1991): 281.
7. Ibid., 282.
8. Katz, *Collection Development*, 92.
9. Harold Bloom, *How to Read and Why* (New York: Scribner, 2000), 22.
10. Richards, "By Your Selection Criteria," 282.
11. E. Vernon Laux, "Looking at Birds, in Meticulous Detail," *New York Times*, September 26, 2000, F5.
12. Charles P. Alexander, "For the Birds," *Time*, June 4, 2001, 66–67.
13. Michael Korda, "Loaded Words," *Brill's Content*, February 2001, 54.
14. James Altas, "Books: Everyone's a Critic," *Brill's Content*, June 2001, 107.
15. Janet Kornblum, "Authors Can Find Critics for Just $295," *USA Today*, May 9, 2001, D3.
16. Josh Chetwynd and Andy Seiler, "In the Film Industry, Everyone's a Critic—Sort Of," *USA Today*, June 25, 2001, D8.
17. Josh Chetwynd, "The Critics Are Raving! And the Studios Are Red-Faced!" *USA Today*, June 25, 2001, D1.
18. Katherine Hobson, "Don't Buy That Blurb: Amazon's Sales Pitch," *U.S. News and World Report*, February 19, 2001, 48.
19. Katz, *Collection Development*, 151.

20. Deirdre Donahue, "Broadway Musical Brings Us Fresh 'Eyre,'" *USA Today*, November 30, 2000, D6.
21. Richard Pevear, "Introduction," in *War and Peace*, by Leo Tolstoy (New York: Knopf, 2007), xiv.
22. Mortimer J. Adler and Charles Van Doren, *How to Read a Book*, rev. and updated (New York: Simon and Schuster, 1972), 32–35.
23. Ibid., 47.

CHAPTER 4

CREATING AND MAINTAINING CORE COLLECTIONS

He writes nothing, whose writings are not read.
—Martial, *Epigrams*

THE PRECEDING CHAPTERS DEAL with the theory and practice of creating adult core collections. This discussion centers on the definition and philosophy of core title selection, the importance of a written collection development statement as a buying plan, and the criteria and sources to use to unearth core titles. It deserves stressing again that there are many different routes a library can take to develop core collections. Collections can be of varying size and cost. Of primary importance is that the core collection reflect the library's community and be viable for its consumers.

The remaining components to be discussed are the actual ordering of titles, budget considerations, evaluation and maintenance of core collections, and the design of a core marketing plan. All these elements play a vital role in selection for the general collection, and they are equally important for core collection development. As always, the ensuing discussion is directed to the specifics of these topics as they relate to core collections.

BUDGET ALLOCATION FOR CORE TITLES

Once the materials budget has been determined, it can then be divided in numerous ways. It can be differentiated by age level (children, teen, adult), format (book, video, audio, e-book), language (English, Spanish, Chinese), or subject (fiction, history, religion) or by whether it is new, retrospective (new to the library but not newly published—useful for tracking collection upgrading), replacement, or core title or, additionally, whether it is a circulating, reference, or electronic resource.

The finer the breakdown of the materials budget, the easier it is for selectors to track their expenditures to ensure that they are following established collection development policies. The resulting list of budget fund levels can become extensive and result in a bookkeeping nightmare for technical services staff. Fortunately, there are many electronic acquisitions systems available today that can support a detailed budget breakdown. The Phoenix Public Library at one point had over 1,500 fund codes. If your library does not have access to an automated fund management system, I suggest that you limit your budget levels to those of the utmost importance. It is a good idea, however, to give each selector unique fund levels to ensure fiscal responsibility. Strong consideration should be given to creating separate fund levels for core materials. These core fund levels allow selectors to see exactly how much money has been spent on core titles, along with the average discount and fill rates.

The percentage of a library's total budget allocated to collection development is an excellent indication of its priorities. Budget allocations should reflect the policies outlined in the collection development statement, with allotments matching the library's needs as expressed therein. Matching funds to a library's stated needs is complicated and can be quite time consuming. However, it is the only way to monitor expenditures and gain a clear picture of how a library is spending its monies. The simplest way to beef up a subject is to allocate funds to it. Allocations need to be reviewed yearly to make certain that the money has been spent as planned and the expected collection results obtained. If collection enhancement has taken place correctly, then funds can be reallocated in the coming fiscal year to another subject area in need of upgrading.

Determining how much money to put in a core budget fund is difficult, particularly if funds are limited. For general subject collections, budget allocations can be determined by reviewing circulation figures, community demands and interests, publication and inflation rates, and proportional subject makeup of bibliographies, such as the two *Public Library Core Collection* volumes or *Subject Guide to Books in Print*. Several of the collection development handbooks listed in chapter 6 have information on setting up a materials budget, including specific formulas for division of monies. None of these, however, is a uniformly accepted method, and all are of limited use in deciding core allocations. In *Collection Development*, William Katz claims that the problem of how to divide a library's materials budget is essentially a "debate between a librarian and an economist. The latter bemoans the lack of statistical data available from libraries; the former counters that libraries (including their budgets) fail to lend themselves to measurement because their books reflect the amazing diversity of human perception."[1] This is certainly the case with core titles.

It is virtually impossible to predict how much money it will take to develop a core collection. Much depends on what emphasis has been placed on collecting basic works and classics in the past, whether these titles have been replaced regularly, and if they are still available for circulation and are in decent condition. Chances are that older library systems already own more core titles, but they may be shabby and worn. A library's definition of *core* and how broadly or narrowly it has been defined in the core development collection statement ultimately determine how many titles need to be purchased to establish this collection.

The easiest way to obtain core funds is simply to trim a percentage off the top of the materials budget for core purchases. This is guaranteed to make waves with the selectors, because it reduces their discretionary selection dollars. If there is staff buy-in to core collection creation, the budget allocation process is a lot less painful for everyone. Ideally, this would be done during a year when the library's materials budget has increased, so the impact on individual branch budgets is less.

Libraries should consider presenting the plans for core collection development to their city councils, library boards, or other official sanctioning bodies, explaining the core's importance to the community and requesting that funds be earmarked for this project. Library Friends groups might be interested in raising additional funds for core collections through their book sales, dinners, or author signings. Cooperative collection development might be undertaken with local community colleges or schools whose budgets have outpaced their facilities and so have additional funding that they cannot spend because of lack of collection space. Additionally, there may be opportunities to apply for grant funds to be used specifically to supplement the materials budget for core collection creation.

Remember, although core collection development is ongoing, the major expenditure comes with the initial purchase of core titles. Once the entire collection has been reviewed and all required core titles purchased, the cost of adding newly published core titles or replacing lost or worn titles is much lower. Once established, the monies for replacement or updating of the core collection need no longer be a separate line item. The funds can now come out of the yearly materials budget, since this upkeep of the core should not be a major ongoing expense. If many additional core titles need to be added every year, then it might be necessary to reexamine the core criteria and selecting practices. Well-selected core titles should retain their significance well beyond two or three years.

Whether these funds are taken from the existing budget or secured elsewhere, they can be divided among agencies or spent centrally. Whichever method is adopted, keep records on how much is being spent on the core—by subject, by each branch, and by the entire system. These figures prove helpful when core collection use is evaluated later to determine if core purchases resulted in any significant changes in circulation. Knowing, for example, exactly how much money has been spent on core titles for a particular subject, staff can then review circulation statistics for that subject to determine if any change has occurred in that subject's use. Consider dividing core funds among the individual branch agencies and the central library. Although this complicates bookkeeping, it results in stronger commitment by the selectors to core list creation, because their funds are being spent on core titles, not some far-off centralized budget over which they have no control.

This occurred in the Phoenix Public Library when funds came from a central pot of money. Librarians attending review forums where core selections were being decided commented that they really did not care which titles were selected as long as the purchases did not come out of their monies. On the other hand, it must be mentioned that having centralized core funds did reduce staff angst about their reduced budgets. It is a trade-off. Each library system has to decide how best to proceed.

When dividing funds among agencies, keep in mind that it is the smallest branch with the most limited budget that most likely needs the most money for core titles. A central library or regional branch with larger collections and accompanying budgets should have many core titles already. It is the smaller collections that need to add more core titles, since, most likely, their coverage of less-in-demand subjects has been limited by budget constraints and reduced shelf space. Large library systems with branches of varying sizes might consider undertaking a tiered core system. In this manner varying amounts of titles are required for agencies, depending on their individual size, budget, or circulation. Although the Phoenix Public Library did adopt a tiered acquisition system for core reference materials, we did not deem it suitable for circulating core titles. We felt that requiring every agency to have the same core titles, with no exceptions, would keep the number of core titles manageable and ensure staff acceptance of the core process. This way everyone had an equal stake in which titles were selected. Most important, it would ultimately limit the core collection to only the best titles; librarians in the smaller branches with budget and size constraints would just not condone designating a mediocre title as core. Allowing the core collection to grow beyond the most outstanding titles would ultimately dilute the collection's value to the community.

The division of the library's collection by subject and genre into an organized buying plan assists you in determining how much money you need to allocate to core collection creation each year. For example, if it is determined that the philosophy collection is weak and missing standard works, more money will need to be allocated when this area is reviewed for core titles. Subject areas such as art and science, with books that are generally more expensive, also require more core dollars. Exactly how much money is needed for any given subject area cannot be determined until the core titles are actually selected and a systemwide inventory undertaken to find out exactly how many copies of a particular core title are needed. At the Phoenix Public Library, we were frequently surprised at the number of titles that were no longer in our collection. Selectors had assumed they still had them. Sometimes the condition or appearance of a core title was so poor that replacement was deemed necessary. New editions with jazzy covers made replacement desirable and resulted in increased circulation. If a branch had several copies of a core title, these were distributed throughout the system to save money. This also expanded access for the out-of-print titles.

If the inability to determine the exact budgetary needs for core selection is too uncomfortable for you, there are various ways to allocate core budgets. Core selection work can proceed during one fiscal year, with the ordering delayed until the next fiscal year after the costs for core selections have been computed. Another possibility is to set aside a finite amount of money for core titles; selections must subsequently match that amount. In this scenario, priorities need to be assigned for each title, because once the core monies are expended, selection ceases. Additionally, libraries can decide not to designate any special funds for the core. Core titles are selected from the regular materials budget with selectors determining core priorities and purchasing accordingly.

This last method is most successful if core selection is deemed a high priority. If it is not, core purchases might be curtailed. This is not a problem if a library is interested in sustaining only a limited core collection. A small, tight selection of the best books available can still enhance a library's collection. The main thing to remember when beginning a core collection is that there is a direct correlation between the money allocated and spent on core titles and the ultimate size of your core collection.

The uncertainty of how much to allocate for core titles can result in too few or too many funds for core purchasing. Surprisingly, both can prove problematic. Obviously, too little money restricts the quantity of titles that can be purchased, possibly resulting in core purchases being postponed until additional funds become available. Although too much core money hardly seems like a problem, excess funding can dilute core collection decisions and result in titles that are not truly worthy of being purchased as core materials. If you should find yourself in such an enviable position, consider buying duplicate copies of the more popular core titles.

Whatever is decided, it is also a good idea to set aside money to purchase the necessary selection tools needed for core work. Additional copies of certain bibliographies, such as *Public Library Core Collection: Fiction* or *Public Library Core Collection: Nonfiction,* might be needed, particularly if selectors throughout the library will be working on core list creation. If your library is fortunate enough to receive a grant or additional funding to pay for core purchases, make certain before you begin expending this money that adequate technical services staff are available to handle the increased ordering, cataloging, and processing needed for core materials. Make certain that you have sufficient processing supplies such as book jackets, DVD cases, or audiobook cases on hand; budget for these increases as well. Check your shelf space to ascertain whether you have enough room to house the additional core titles. If not, and if purchasing more shelves is not an option, consider doing a massive deselection project before receiving your first core shipment.

ORDERING CORE TITLES SYSTEMWIDE

In small library systems of only one or two agencies, once a title has been determined to be core, it can basically just be ordered. Although core ordering has an impact on any size library, in larger systems it has greater ramifications. If not organized properly, ordering can cause havoc in the normal selection process and create substantial additional work for selectors. To keep this to a minimum, some central work needs to be done up front even in libraries without centralized selection.

It is a good idea to coordinate core subject ordering with general add and replacement work in the same subject. This approach allows selectors to know, for example, that they are required to buy a certain book on pandas. They might, therefore, elect to skip another noncore title on the same subject. To save selector time, searching systemwide for title availability can be done centrally if staffing allows, and holdings information can then be supplied directly on selection lists. This approach saves each agency having to check its holdings and circulation for every core title. Even if this initial checking is done centrally, it still is important that branch staff check their shelves for the core title's condition. Knowing which titles they already have allows branch staff to check only those titles their branch is listed as owning. Preparing selection lists in call number order assists this shelf check.

When doing ongoing core review work—after the initial purchase of core titles—staff continue to save time by following these same procedures. It is far more effective to have all core selectors conform to the same core add and replacement schedule; see figure 5.2 below for a sample breakdown of the entire collection into three mostly equal parts. Such a schedule allows a core selection list to be released approximately ten times over the course of a year. Adhering to a core replacement schedule ultimately saves staff time because it eliminates checking individually for title availability and repeatedly writing or creating online the same order. Technical services staff will appreciate not having to purchase, catalog, and process the same titles over and over again. Schedule exceptions may need to be made for those titles that are lost almost immediately or are in such demand that staff members do not want to wait for the core ordering cycle to repeat itself. Even in these cases, however, whenever a core title is ordered it should be offered for purchase systemwide on the off chance that another agency also needs a replacement.

ACQUISITION OF CORE TITLES

Locating and acquiring core titles should mirror the normal acquisition procedures used to purchase titles for the general collection. The closer core purchasing is to established library processes, the less impact it has on the work flow of technical services and the less likely it is to cause a delay in receipt of library materials. Create core orders in a manner consistent with the rest of library purchasing. Communication between selectors and technical services staff is crucial to the success of any core collection project. Besides just normal courtesy between library units, talking to technical services staff about the forthcoming core collection can help ensure that these materials are received in a timely manner and can eliminate potential resentment on the part of either public services or technical services staffs. To this end, the buying plan schedule needs to be developed in conjunction with acquisitions, cataloging, and processing units. If you have decided to develop a special core work form that will ultimately be used by technical services to order core titles, this needs to be approved by technical services staff before core selectors begin to use it.

Acquisitions staff, with their experience and expertise in purchasing materials, are an excellent resource for determining publisher reliability, discounts, and fill rates. This is useful information because classic titles can be available in numerous editions. Often acquisitions staff are also knowledgeable about special vendor purchasing plans or new publishing imprints. Most libraries use a vendor (or jobber; the two names are used interchangeably today) to eliminate the need to order every title individually from its publisher. Vendors allow libraries to place orders for titles from many different publishers at the same time, often with a substantial prenegotiated discount.

Once acquisitions staff are alerted to the advent of core collection development and the type of material to be ordered, they may deem it worthwhile to talk to the library's vendors or directly to publishers about the implementation of core purchasing. Acquisitions staff may be able to obtain an additional discount with certain publishers that are known to publish classics or core titles regularly. If there has been a significant increase in the book budget because of core allocations or a grant for core purchasing, acquisitions may decide that an increase in vendor discounts is justified and negotiate accordingly. Vendor discounts are usually determined by the total amount of money to be spent with one particular vendor.

With selector input, acquisitions staff can set up an approval plan or standing order for ongoing receipt of potential core purchases. For example, the Library of America Series books are excellent, reasonably priced editions of outstanding American writings printed on acid-free paper. This series could be established as a standing order, so that each new title is automatically sent to the library. If a library needs multiple copies, the standing order can be set up for this as well. Acquisitions can also arrange for samples of different editions, new publisher imprints, or binding alternatives to be sent to the library for selector review.

Processing and mending staff can assist core selection by recommending the most durable editions of a core title. This is an important consideration, because longevity and retention rates can save money. Unlike the selection of best-sellers, for which there are usually no options, core selection frequently allows for binding, imprint, and publisher choices. Public services librarians need to remember to take advantage of the knowledge available in the library's technical services department. Too often, selectors do not talk to their acquisitions and cataloging colleagues about their collection needs.

OUT-OF-PRINT PURCHASING

Sad as it is to relate, core and classic titles do go out of print. One would assume that core titles would remain in print indefinitely, since by their very nature they have lasting appeal and continued importance. This is true up to a point and does work in the favor of the core selector, but far too many excellent core books have gone out of print. Katz reports in *Collection Development* that "one study found, both in Britain and the United States, after 10 years less than half the original publication is recorded as remaining in print."[2] The ALA Notable Books Committee, which since 1944 has been selecting the outstanding books of the year, was pleased to discover that Notable Books did stay in print longer than the average title. In 1996 the committee found that 34 percent of the titles selected in 1946 were still available, usually in a reprinted edition. Fifty percent of the titles from 1956, 48 percent of the titles from 1966, 66 percent of the titles from 1976, and 68 percent of the titles from 1986 were still in print.[3]

The benefits of acquiring a desired out-of-print item are obvious, particularly a core book, because only the best and most desirable titles would have been deemed core—a book should not be deemed obsolete and expendable merely because it has gone out of print. One of the most important functions libraries perform for their community is continuing to stock books that are no longer available elsewhere. The popularity of book clubs, with their loyalty to reading good books and the classics, has helped keep these titles in print longer. The advent of the e-book has helped too. Although most current titles are readily available on Kindle, the same cannot be said for its weak backlist. It is "strangely spotty." Although you can download John Updike's posthumous book *Endpoint,* currently you cannot buy *Rabbit Run* or any of the other Rabbit titles, two of them Pulitzer Prize winners and likely core titles.[4] We can only hope that this situation will change as more titles are added and the demand increases.

Until recently, the acquisition of out-of-print books was labor intensive, expensive, and something most public libraries just ignored completely. The ongoing advances in digital technology have eliminated the difficulty of obtaining out-of-print books. This is a tremendous boon to collection development and especially to core collections. The evolution of the Internet and proliferation of online used-book store websites have made out-of-print titles readily available. Online sources such as Amazon and Alibris can now expedite the acquisition of these titles. Used-book dealers and even thrift stores such as Goodwill list their used books on Amazon, many of them out of print or out of stock from standard vendors, including Amazon itself, and often at a fraction of the original list price. Each of the title listings available from Amazon suppliers provides details on the book's condition along with the vendor's customer satisfaction rating.

Founded in 1998, Alibris is an online service that provides access to over 100 million used, new, out-of-stock, and out-of-print books along with music and movies from over 1,400 independent sellers. Alibris has a separate library department that accepts library purchase orders, guarantees the condition of each book, and searches for specific titles using its Want List Matching System. All libraries, no matter their size, need to create procedures that enable them to partake of this new vendor technology so as to ensure that their core collections remain complete despite a title being out of print.

Print on demand (POD), sometimes called publish on demand, is another possibility for acquiring out-of-print or out-of-stock titles. This technology keeps a title on a computer database, and new copies are not printed until an order has been received. POD is a step beyond the digital repository of titles, such as Google Book Project or the electronic niche "self-publishers" Xlibris or IUniverse (see chapter 1), in that it also supplies the actual book production. With the advent of POD, publishers can now keep books in print indefinitely no matter how few copies they sell. Not surprising, one of the leading service POD providers is Amazon, which claims that it can now print and bind a book in less than two hours through its Book Surge division. Both Baker and Taylor's Replica Books and Ingram's Lightning Source can also supply POD titles for library core collections. Although POD has been around for about ten years, it has been slow to catch on with libraries, for these books cost more per unit than a conventional print run and the resulting copy is often not as slick and finished as those from traditional printing, often arriving without a dust jacket or limited cover art. Librarians should always ascertain beforehand the quality of a specific POD company's product before ordering any title. Still, core selectors should be aware of this option when looking to purchase a title that is out of print and have procedures in place to purchase POD copies if the need arises.

Once it is determined that a core title is not available through a library's usual acquisition methods, measures need to be in place to begin searching further for this book. As we have seen, it is no longer necessary to determine whether a title is truly out of print; this is a nonissue today. What is important is the preferred next step to acquiring the title. For example, a library might decide to work directly with a specific out-of-print vendor such as Alibris for Libraries or even to purchase all core titles directly from a vendor known to handle more out-of-stock and out-of-print titles. If this is not successful, then a library needs to decide if it wishes to pursue POD as well. The decision to purchase out-of-print materials has ramifications for acquisitions staff time, for selectors, and for the state of the collection as well as the library's book budget. Therefore, it is important to set up guidelines for out-of-print selection and acquisition, and to include these in the core collection development policy.

Purchasing out-of-print books should be a part of any core collection, no matter its size or scope. Whether these core titles are acquired through an out-of-print online vendor, through a POD supplier, or as an e-book, there are few reasons remaining to omit these titles from your core collection.

LABELING CORE TITLES

When establishing a core collection, librarians need to think about whether they wish to label these titles as "core" physically on the book or audiovisual item and in the catalog. If you are planning a marketing campaign with these titles (see below), you might consider adding "core" to the call number or perhaps using a separate core label on the spine or outside of the book. A core spine label helps the public spot these titles on the shelves and alerts staff not to weed them but to notice if condition warrants ordering a replacement copy. Circulation staff can also easily determine that a damaged title is core and alert appropriate selection staff to reorder. Tagging core titles in your catalog or database helps the public find them, and it also helps selectors create core selection lists or book lists; most electronic catalogs can sort titles by several different fields, including call numbers. Missing and lost title reports are often created in call number order, and core titles, identified as such, would sort together, allowing for ease in replacement work. In this manner, statistical reports on core title use can also be established to assist core evaluation, to allow selectors to determine circulation of core titles compared to the general collection, or to keep track of the size of the core collection. If you decide to label core titles, be sure to discuss this with technical services, for it is the rare processing section that welcomes yet another spine label. Processing staff need to be alerted to the core collection before core books arrive, so that their procedures are in place and adequate core labels are on hand. If retrospective labeling of core titles already in the library also needs to be done, technical services must determine the best method to ensure consistency throughout the library system.

Although core books can be shelved separately, I do not advise this, because it creates an extra place to look for a particular title. But if you do decide to separate core titles, it is crucial that the call number or location code in the library's database indicate that the title is core. A core label assists library shelvers and staff when creating special core title displays. At the Phoenix Public Library we discovered that library users picked up on the core designation and actually went looking for these titles knowing that they were of excellent quality. The public seemed to appreciate the assistance this labeling supplied. For the same reasons, it also helped public services staff to assist library patrons in finding the best titles on any given subject. Unfortunately, such labeling and tagging create more work for technical services at the time of book or audiovisual receipt, and later, if a title ceases to be core, additional steps are involved in removing its core indicator and moving it to the general collection.

MAINTAINING THE CORE COLLECTION

Once a core collection has been established, its maintenance is quite straightforward. It requires a systematic reexamination to ascertain that core titles are still being used and of continuing interest to the community served. After the initial review of the entire adult collection has been completed and all needed core titles ordered, it is time to begin to reconsider the entire core collection. Ideally, core collection creation does not take an inordinate amount of time, and the next phase of review and maintenance of the core collection can begin within a reasonable time frame.

The establishment of core collections in fiction and all subject areas should not take longer than four years. Much like the rest of a library's practices, core collection maintenance and evaluation need to be ongoing; allowing too much time between review cycles can result in collections that become depleted, run-down, or of limited appeal. The appearance of the core collection reflects the importance the library places on it. Core titles should complement and enhance the rest of the collection. It is a good idea to keep a centralized list of core titles that is continuously updated as literary prizes are awarded or whenever new bibliographies and book lists are issued or revised. Although the core update committee might decide not to include a prize winner, having the information readily available for the next review cycle simplifies and greatly speeds that process.

The Phoenix Public Library had an elaborate system of yearly add and replacement committee work, and core collection maintenance was added to this already established process. The library had divided its entire nonfiction adult collection into three equal parts. Fiction was also divided into three equal sections by using *Public Library Core Collection: Fiction* as a guide to determine approximately how many titles were in each portion of the alphabet. In this way the complete adult collection, including the core collection, was reviewed every three years. Implementing core review in tandem with add and replacement work is logical. Because librarians are examining subject bibliographies, checklists, publisher catalogs, reviews, and the existing collection to replace lost or outdated titles for the general collection, it makes sense to have these same selectors evaluate core titles at the same time.

Each adult services librarian in the Phoenix Public Library system was given committee subject assignments at the beginning of the fiscal year. In anticipation of this process, clerical staff checked every core title centrally to find out if it still was in print. Systemwide holdings and circulation were also checked. The collection development office distributed the previous core lists, now three years old, to the core committee members along with the updated circulation and publishing information. Additional bibliography and book list citings as well as prizes awarded since the core list was first created were also distributed to committee members.

This is a fine time for the core review committee members to reread the core collection development buying plan in order to reexamine the original core criteria and make certain that they still are appropriate. Any proposed changes to core criteria need to be made at this time. Procedures for their approval and implementation should have been established before the review process; ideally, these policies have been outlined in the core collection selection policy statement.

Next, core committee members need to evaluate every core title to make certain that it continues to be suitable for the library's users. This is accomplished by reviewing standard bibliographies, often the revised editions of the ones used in the initial creation of the core collection. Does the title still appear in *Public Library Core Collection* volumes? Is it now listed in any new book lists? Is it your community's Big Read book? Has it perhaps won a recent literary prize? Is it still talked about and used as a comparison when similar titles are discussed? On the other hand, has the title been discredited? Is it outdated? Is there a newer edition or a recently published title that is better?

A decision to remove or add a title always needs to be made cautiously. It is an expensive proposition to mandate that every branch discard an existing core title or require that one core title be replaced with another. If the difference between the new title and the original core selection is slight, the newer or updated core title can be recommended rather than required for purchase. In this way branches can decide on their own if they want to spend their money to update the core collection. In Phoenix, selectors often elected to buy these newer titles. If agencies no longer had the original title, then they were obligated to buy the newly recommended title. Proceeding with the same criteria used during the initial core list creation, selectors can unearth new core titles and add them to existing core collections. Certainly all the recent Pulitzer, Nobel, and National Book Award winners over the past three years should be considered for inclusion. The changes made to the existing core collection during this review process should affect no more than 5 to 10 percent of the initial core title list. A greater change warrants a review of the library's original core criteria unless the library has revised its collection development statement significantly or decided to expand its core collection. Admittedly, there might be a few more changes necessary after the first review, as selectors were just beginning to learn the rudiments of core selection when the initial core titles were chosen.

It cannot be stressed enough that well-selected core titles circulate, though perhaps not as much as a current best-seller or an Oprah title. Committee members must review each core title's circulation to make sure it still holds interest and importance for the library's clientele. To assist in this review process, librarians can set a minimum circulation rate required for all core titles. These rates can be the same for all subjects and every agency, or they can vary. A busy branch might demand a higher circulation of its core titles than a smaller branch where turnover rates are generally lower. Core titles in high-demand subject areas, such as sports, crafts, or biography, might have an assigned circulation rate higher than titles in philosophy, history, or law, for example. At the Phoenix Public Library, we required that every core title circulate at least five times in every agency during any given year. We assumed that each core title was in good condition and attractive. It is not fair to expect shabby classic titles to compete with their newer, splashy general collection cousins. A number of new, attractive core books were purchased to replace old, shopworn copies. We wanted to give every core title a fair chance at snaring library users' interest.

During this review process, the Phoenix Public Library no longer held regular core forums for all librarians to discuss and vote on every recommended core title. Core decisions were made solely by the committees, though drafts of core selection lists with changes and updates were sent to all selectors for their review before the final list was issued. New core titles had brief information or an annotation explaining why the title had been added. During the following three years of the review cycle, a yearly meeting was held to solicit selector input and to discuss the entire core collection process. Once all the librarians' suggestions were discussed and agreed upon by the core committee, a core selection list was distributed to all agencies.

As I mentioned earlier, in the Phoenix Public Library, this core review was done in conjunction with general add and replacement work. Core titles were interfiled in Dewey order with general add and replacement titles, but they were clearly marked as core. This simplified selection because librarians had to deal with only one list. Selectors could easily see whether a subject had a required core purchase and so could elect to pass on buying a noncore title on the same subject.

Upon receipt of this updated core selection list, selectors examined each core title's condition. The list noted whether the branch already had a title, again making replacement work easier. If the committee had decided to withdraw a title from the core collection, a separate list was sent to every agency for ease in deselection. The individual agency then made the decision whether to retain the title in the regular collection, removing the spine core labels as warranted. Technical services was also given a copy of the withdrawn-from-core list, so that its staff could change the online catalog to reflect this global change. Librarians do not have the authority to remove or deselect any core title unless condition warrants it. In this case a replacement copy needs to be expeditiously ordered. Librarians can, however, petition the core committee and request that a title be deleted or added to the core, ensuring the consistency and integrity of the core collection throughout the library system.

CORE MARKETING PLAN

After three long years of enormous staff time and energy devoted to developing a core collection of the finest literature, it would be a shame if this marvelous new collection was not highlighted or its merits not understood by the library's clientele. The art of selection is a mystery to the general public, but most of them are somewhat intrigued by the process. Whether they read classics or not, members of the community—the city council, school boards, and other civic organizations—will be pleased to hear that the library has made a commitment to enhancing its collection along traditional lines. This can serve as an excellent public relations tool to answer groups that are concerned with the overall quality of the collection. A brand-new core collection is a perfect time to capitalize on this interest. No library should waste the opportunity to gain additional community support and positive publicity for its collection.

There are countless ways to promote core collections. In libraries where adult programming is up and running successfully, it is not much of a stretch to develop programs that focus on core titles. A classic or great book discussion group could be started using core titles. The series could begin with Italo Calvino's thought-provoking essay *Why Read the Classics?*[5] In a lecture series on the classics, the local professors who helped with core selection and attended the library's core forums could be invited to talk about their selections and why they are important. A library could sponsor a film series using movies made from classics or develop a series of film talks on whether classic books make classic films. Libraries might contact publishers of core title authors to see if any of these authors would be available to speak. Local celebrities might also be invited to share their favorite books. Poetry workshops, subject lecture series—the possibilities are truly endless. Any of these programming ideas could be packaged, a grant proposal written, and special funding sought.

Whether a library decides to implement special programming to tout core titles or not, there are numerous other ways to promote the collection. Every library should, at the very least, write a press release about its core collection that can additionally be used as a presentation to the library board, Friends groups, or the city council; see figure 4.1 for a sample. Remember that your library's news release must compete with many other organizations' press releases. Anything you can do to make your copy stand out from the others can result in your event being publicized. Make sure your release is accurate, honest, clear, and concise. Every press release should answer the five "w" questions: Whom is the announcement about? What is the announcement about? Where is the event or service taking place? When is the event or service taking place? Why might the public be interested in what is being announced?[6] The release should be sent to the local media—newspapers and magazines, television and radio stations—and particularly to the editors, reviewers, newscasters, or reporters who have written book-related pieces in the past. A follow-up phone call can help draw attention to your release. The press release announcing the new core collection can also be tied into a program series or special exhibit. At the Phoenix Public Library's Central Library, we displayed unusual rare and first editions of core titles from our Art of the Book Room to publicize this new collection. The exhibit provided a photo opportunity that appealed to

FIGURE 4.1

SAMPLE PRESS RELEASE

FOR IMMEDIATE RELEASE

Contact:
Mario Jerry, Public Information Officer
Southwest Public Library
53 West Saguaro Blvd
Anytown, AZ 85062
(602) 555-4660

Southwest Library Getting Back to Basics

Anytown, Ariz. What do *Mein Kampf, Pride and Prejudice, Casablanca, Star Wars,* and *Gone with the Wind* have in common? Although this is an unlikely combination of classic literature and films to be lumped together, each is part of the library's new core collection. Core books and films are the titles that have altered the course of history, like Marx's *Communist Manifesto* and *Quotations from Chairman Mao.* Others have illuminated our lives, like Sigmund Freud's *Interpretation of Dreams* and Alex Comfort's *Joy of Sex.* Still others are films that changed the way we view the world, such as *Schindler's List* and *Dr. Strangelove.* All are very different, but all are of the first rank and of lasting importance. It is the library's intention to go back to the very foundation of the library, to the basics of what makes a library a library. The creation of the core collection took over three years, and titles were selected by librarians throughout the Southwest Public Library with supporting grants from the Two Bank Foundation.

A complete collection of these landmark films and books is now available for checkout at every single branch library and the central library. Titles are clearly labeled "core" for ease of use. So if are you tired of sitting in front of a computer screen all day or have always wanted to read the classics and see the great films, now is the perfect time. Stop by your neighborhood branch and check the core collection out!

For additional information about the Southwest Public Library and for current library hours, call (602) 555-7890.

----

the newspaper and resulted in some excellent publicity for the core collection and the library.

Each core committee was asked to choose ten to fifteen titles from its assigned subject or fiction area. Lists of these core titles were printed and distributed. This was an expeditious way to develop book lists, because selectors were familiar with the titles—they had just evaluated them for core inclusion. The lists were issued as bookmarks celebrating good reading and were available about the same time as the core books arrived at the branches and the Central Library. Copies of several of the book lists were added to the press release sent to the newspaper and were printed there.

Libraries can also add these lists of recommended core titles to their website. The public could be asked for their opinion of the core titles and for suggestions of titles that the librarians may have missed. Libraries can participate in county fairs and street festivals touting the core collection. A table or booth stocked with library handouts and core book lists is an excellent way to publicize the newly established core collection. The publicity possibilities are limited only by your imagination, so enjoy creating programs and book lists that support the finest literature and good reading.

Chapter 6 includes some general guides that provide suggestions for programs along with complete publicity plans, including how to write a press release with samples. The completion of a core collection is an excellent time to generate positive feedback for the library and for reading and to ensure that core titles are used. Don't let this opportunity slip away.

Notes

1. William A. Katz, *Collection Development: The Selection of Materials for Libraries* (New York: Holt, 1980), 66.
2. Ibid., 177.
3. Sandy Whiteley, ed., *50 Years of Notable Books* (Chicago: American Library Association, Reference and Adult Services Division, 1996), v.
4. Charles McGrath, "A By-the-Book Reader Meets the Machine," *New York Times*, May 28, 2009, Weekend 23.
5. Italo Calvino, *Why Read the Classics?* trans. Martin McLaughlin (New York: Pantheon, 1999), 3–9.
6. Rashelle S. Karp, ed., *Powerful Public Relations: A How-To Guide for Libraries* (Chicago: American Library Association, 2002), 9.

CHAPTER 5

IMPLEMENTING THE CORE COLLECTION

The best reading for the largest number at the least cost.
—Melvil Dewey

ONCE THE CRITERIA TO be used in making core decisions and the importance of keeping track of the specifics on every core candidate are understood, the question that arises is how to manage the continuous flow of new title information and retain the necessary core information for updating purposes.

TRACKING SYSTEM FOR CORE TITLES

Many libraries utilize some type of selection work form, whether it be paper or online, to order books and other materials. Ideally, these forms are multipurpose and can be used by different staff members through the entire selection cycle. Selectors may use them initially to write up or designate promising titles in order to keep track of these potential purchases and then, ultimately, to place the orders. Between these two events, clerical staff may handle these forms to complete citation verification or create selection order lists.

Wherever possible, repetition of order writing and duplication of forms should be avoided. Existing order forms must be flexible enough to work for core title information retention and purchasing too. If an established form is used for core collection development, it must be clearly labeled as such. Different treatment and additional purchasing options, such as using an out-of-print vendor like Alibris, may be necessary to obtain core titles. Cataloging and processing staff also need to be notified whenever a core title is being ordered, so that a core designation is included in the call number, in the online catalog, and on the item label.

Some librarians might prefer to create a unique form just for core titles; others might prefer to track core titles entirely online or utilize downloaded information from Books in Print, Title Source, or Amazon. There is no preferred method as long as the procedure is easy to use and provides all the needed information for both selectors and technical services staff. That decision rests solely on the individual library, though consistency within a library system is strongly advised. For the purposes of our discussion, it makes no difference whether the selection work form is paper or electronic.

My preference is always to work with an existing form; one thing most libraries do not need is another form. If a new form is created, it should be similar in style to the general selection form but clearly designated as a core selection form to avoid staff confusion. A sample of the Phoenix Public Library's book selection work form is shown in figure 5.1. For over twenty years this form was used for all selection functions. Today many of the library's selection processes are done online, and the form is used only occasionally; however, it may prove useful for libraries that have not yet developed a selection work form or for those wishing to update an existing form or create one online.

Whatever format your library ultimately decides to use to track core titles, the following list includes all the pertinent information needed for core selection and acquisition:

Bibliographic Details

Include all the basics—call number, title, author, publisher, price, publication date, and ISBN. If a particular imprint, translation, or specific cover art is sought, then this information needs to be given along with the publisher and whether hardcover or paperback is requested. Make sure that the ISBN matches the desired edition.

Title Credentials

Make note of wherever the title appears—for example, one of the *Public Library Core Collection* volumes or R. R. Bowker's *Reader's Adviser* (no longer updated, but still extremely useful for core collections). If you are creating a new form, these basic bibliographies could be listed directly on the form and simply checked off or circled to save staff time and to provide a visual reminder to selectors to verify titles in these sources. Provide sufficient space for notes to enable selectors to list all pertinent "hit" information, such as Nobel Prize or National Book Award winners. Review and bibliography citations should always be correctly and completely noted, so that librarians can review a title's credentials personally. As a time saver in Phoenix we developed our own list of abbreviations for the major review sources used in core selection—for example, *Publishers Weekly* (PW), *Library Journal* (LJ), and *Kirkus Reviews* (K).

FIGURE 5.1

SAMPLE BOOK SELECTION WORK CARD FOR TRACKING CORE TITLES

RUSH				**BOOK SELECTION WORK CARD**				
ISBN #						SELECTOR		
AUTHOR								
TITLE								
PUB. CAT. #				CD	DVD	SO	OTHER	
REVIEW SOURCE			PUBLISHER				PUB. DATE	
							PRICE	
DYNIX Y / N	ED	REF	CIRC	NEW	CALL NO.		NOTES:	
OO Y / N	FUND			ADD				
B&T Y / N								
BIP Y / N	LOCATION			PAP				
GIFT/MEM				PRLB				
CEN_____AC_____CE_____CH_____DS_____HA_____IR_____								
JN_____ME_____OC_____PV_____SA_____YU_____								

The abbreviations at the bottom of this three-part form used by selectors in the Phoenix Public Library represent each of the branches and the Central Library. This space was used to record holdings of a particular title for each agency.

Other abbreviations are
Y / N: Yes, No

OO: On order

B&T: Baker and Taylor availability

BIP: Books in Print

MEM: Memorial gift

SO: Standing order

PRLB: Review copy available

Acquisitions Notes

If a particular edition is desired, a brief note alerting acquisitions to this prefer-ence will assist in getting the correct edition for the library. If the publisher is an unusual one that the library does not use often, listing the address or phone number or both is essential. If the title is out of print, this needs to be noted. An out-of-print designation alerts the acquisitions staff immediately that this title needs to be handled differently and eliminates the wasted effort of sending the order through the library's usual vendor. If the core title is sold by Amazon or Alibris, this should be indicated. Or if a selector has seen the item listed in an individual out-of-print dealer's catalog, the dealer's phone number, website, and the book's order number should accompany the order. If a selector has seen the title in a bookstore, particularly on the remainder or sale tables, this too should be noted. Acquisitions staff could call the bookstore and have the book sent directly to the library. Often these remainder titles are out of print or out of stock and, if ordered through normal jobber channels, after some delay will result in a publisher-out-of-stock report rather than an acquired core title. If it is recommended that the title be ordered directly from the publisher, this too should be noted. Ultimately, acquisitions staff make purchasing decisions based on their experience, but any help selectors can supply results in faster title receipt. Selectors should give all the pertinent information to acquisitions and then step back and allow staff to do the job they are trained to do.

Systemwide Holdings

All library agencies can be preprinted on each core tracking form with enough room to add holdings/copy information and circulation figures for each branch and the central library. These data assist core committees in their review work and enable circulation and holdings information to appear on the final core selection list, which saves librarian time systemwide. A well-developed core tracking form can make selectors' work easier and more efficient.

Whether they are paper or electronic, selection work forms need to be main-tained and kept up to date even when a core subject lies "dormant," awaiting its next review within the three-year cycle. Selectors in libraries that have core collections or those that are developing them should always be on the lookout for potential core additions. After a title receives an award or is cited repeatedly as the best book written on a given subject, a tracking form can be filled out immediately and added to the other core candidates awaiting consideration. A review might say something like, "This title replaces [a title currently on the core list] as the most important work in this field." In this case a note should be added to the core list suggesting the possibility of replacing the current core title with this new one. Libraries should not wait to order a potential core title until its subject comes up for review but should purchase it immediately for the general collection. If it is eventually added to the core collection, libraries that already own it can pass on ordering it and just label the existing copy as core. You do not want your library users to wait three years for a well-reviewed title. When you are considering this title for core collection inclusion, circulation information will already be available to assist the evaluation.

REVIEW OF THE CORE collection is best done centrally for the entire system, although every librarian should be encouraged to participate and submit potential core titles throughout the review cycle. In smaller library systems, individual selectors may be assigned ongoing core duties. Maintaining core information on an ongoing basis prevents overlooking an important core candidate later and saves selectors having to survey several years of reviews and lists during the actual scheduled core review period.

Please remember that I am not talking about hundreds of new titles yearly. By its very definition a core title should remain timeless, so yearly additions to the core should be slight. If core work is done accurately, there also will be few core deletions. True core titles should continue to circulate year after year. This is different from the general collection; studies have shown that a new book is used most heavily during its first year in library collections and that over 95 percent of the collection ages so quickly that after four or five years these items no longer circulate at all.[1]

CORE SCHEDULE AND TIME FRAME

A three-year cycle for core collection review is recommended. This means that each core title is reviewed for appropriateness, circulation, and actual physical condition at least once every three years. Although the ideal would be to review the entire collection every year, this is hardly realistic. A systematic reconsideration of core items must be done regularly or the collection may become static and unused. If a title is truly a core title, it will still be circulating even after three years on a library's shelves.

There is no hard-and-fast time frame for completing a total analysis of a library's collection. The division of a collection into three fairly equal parts should prove satisfactory and doable for most libraries. The division of the collection into three allows for approximately one core list and accompanying forum per month with a little breathing room for holidays or busy summer schedules. Figure 5.2 is a sample breakdown of the entire Dewey range, along with the subjects covered, that libraries can follow in reviewing their core collections. This breakdown of the entire adult collection is based on the size of the regular collection, not the intended size of the core collection. No matter what the ultimate size of the library's core collection, selectors must still search through the entire collection looking for potential core candidates. At the Phoenix Public Library we found that this pattern dovetailed well with our annual add and replacement review.

FIGURE 5.2

SAMPLE BREAKDOWN OF DEWEY DECIMAL SYSTEM FOR CORE COLLECTION REVIEW

First Year

000; 100	Generalities; Philosophy; Psychology
200	Religion
300–319; 360–369	Social Issues
370–399	Education; Folklore
630–649	Domestic Sciences; Pets
930–939; 950–969	World History
Biography A–E	
Fiction A–F	
Science Fiction	

Second Year

320–329; 340–349; 350–359	Political Science; Law
500–559	Physical Science; Math
610–619	Medicine
780–799	Performing Arts; Music; Sports
800	Literature
900–919; 940–949	Geography; European History
Biography F–L; 920–929	Collected Biography; Genealogy
Fiction G–O	
Romance	
Western	

Third Year

330–339; 650–659	Business and Economics
400	Language
560–599	Natural Science
600–609; 620–629; 660–699	Engineering; Construction
700–779	Art
970–999	American History
Biography M–Z	
Fiction P–Z	
Mystery	

The time frame for core collection development work and for the yearly ongoing review needs to be established as early as possible in the buying year to give selectors, their supervisors, and administrators enough lead time to schedule meetings and to accomplish all the necessary core work. It is recommended that core assignments be handed out as soon as the materials budget has been approved and the core allocation established. As most city budgets are based on a fiscal year, rather than the calendar year, core schedules would follow this scheme as well.

Ideally, preparation for core review should begin about six months before the start of the fiscal year. For example, if the new fiscal year is scheduled to begin on July 1, then core updating work, which includes the checking of holdings, availability, and circulation, would commence the February before. Then in May, before the new budget year begins, core selectors would be queried about their assignment preference, so they are ready to resume core review as soon as the funds are allocated. The earlier that selectors receive their core assignments, the more time they have to work on them and the better their decisions will be. This also gives supervisors an idea of which of their librarian staff will be most involved with core work, enabling them to schedule staff time equitably and to add to a selector's performance review specific goals related to core list completion dates. It is a good idea to establish a schedule for core committee and core forum meetings during May or June, too. The entire librarian staff should be given these meeting dates well in advance to avoid scheduling conflicts with other projects and to ensure good attendance at the core meetings. Remember to book the necessary meeting rooms.

Core work would begin the February before the fiscal year. Figure 5.3 shows a sample time frame for core review and one committee's work schedule for an established portion of the core collection. Throughout the fiscal year the rest of the core committees would also be meeting on a staggered schedule and following a similar time frame. This is, of course, only a guide. Each library will need to adjust the time frame to suit its own staffing needs, budget, and schedule idiosyncrasies. But let me stress again the importance of allowing all core selectors ample time for core work and giving every librarian an opportunity to propose core list changes and react to the list before it is finalized for selection. This is the only way to develop a high-quality list and to continue to have staff input for core collections.

If a library is just beginning core work and wants to include core forums in the process, it can adapt this sample time frame to meet these first-time needs by adding forum meetings to the schedule and allowing more time for each committee to compile the initial core lists. A good rule is to allow at least two to three weeks for selectors in agencies to review the draft of the core list before a core forum. As you might imagine, creating the initial core lists takes more time than merely reviewing established core lists. Sufficient time should be allowed for every librarian to react to the draft of every core list before it is finalized. During this initial time frame there is, of course, no need to schedule core title reexamination, since no core titles have been selected yet. Therefore, core committee work can begin sooner to allow plenty of staff time to develop the basic core collection. Needless to say, core committee work begins only after the core collection policy statement has been written and approved.

DIVERSITY OF CORE TITLES

A library's core collection, like the rest of its collection, must meet the particular needs of that library's clientele. Reading local newspapers and magazines can help selectors become aware of the interests, characteristics, and organizations that make their library's community unique. There are differences in

---

FIGURE 5.3

SAMPLE TIME FRAME FOR CORE REVIEW

February

Analysis of existing core titles to be reviewed this coming year begins.

Core titles checked to see if they are still available through primary vendor.

Designated standard bibliographies of recommended titles checked for core titles.

Branch holdings and circulation for every core title noted.

Recommended core candidates added to core title review.

(These tasks ideally could be done by central clerical staff; if none available, work could be assigned to staff throughout the system.)

May

Selectors queried as to their core assignment preferences.

Forthcoming year's core review schedule distributed.

Librarians and all staff members asked for recommendations of additions to and deletions from existing core lists.

June

Core committee and Dewey call number assignments given to librarians and their supervisors.

Completed core reexamination and results sent to appropriate core selectors.

Committee and forum meeting schedule established.

the collection needs, for example, of libraries in rural communities and those in urban or suburban areas. Earlier I used the unique desert setting of the Phoenix Public Library to illustrate this basic point by explaining the necessity of buying only those gardening books that were appropriate for the most arid of conditions. In that case, the library would be justified in not purchasing as a core title an award-winning book published by the Royal Rose Society of England, where it rains almost every day. This example may be obvious, but not so clear-cut is how to ensure that core collections reflect the cultural and racial diversity of the community the library serves. These decisions are more difficult.

An analysis of the 2000 U.S. census showed that the most striking aspect of the changes in this nation's racial and ethnic makeup during the previous

Meeting rooms booked.

Core budget determined and fund codes created.

July

Selectors begin their core work assignments.

Committee members research core possibilities and evaluate data in order to update existing core list.

September

First core committee meets to discuss additions to and deletions from its portion of the core collection.

October

Draft of core list with changes sent to all librarians for their final input.

November

Core changes sent to administrators for their approval.

Finalized core selection list sent to all agencies.

Separate list of titles that are no longer core also sent.

December

Librarians in agencies examine their collections and determine which core titles need to be ordered or replaced.

Decisions made about whether to retain or discard titles that are no longer core.

January

Systemwide core orders compiled and given to acquisitions staff for purchase.

decade was speed, with Hispanic and Asian populations spreading from the West and Southwest to all fifty states. The number of states that were overwhelmingly populated by non-Hispanic whites in the census had shrunk. A decade earlier, fourteen states, most of them in the north, had populations of more than 89 percent non-Hispanic white; in 2000 there were just four: North Dakota, Iowa, West Virginia, and Maine.[2] All of this in less than ten years. In 2010 the next census will be completed and will most likely show a continuation of this trend. Librarians must pay attention to these population shifts as they impact their communities and ultimately their collections.

The nation's library users come from many different cultures, and they are constantly on the move; viable core collections must address the multiculturalism prevalent throughout the country as well as in the immediate community served. How does a selector ensure that the library's core collection mirrors the ethnicity of its users? Initially, the library must determine exactly which cultures currently make up its clientele. All selectors should have this information at their fingertips. A brief summary of the census data outlining the community's diverse population groups can be included in the collection development policy statement. Additionally, the core collection should include titles that reflect the many immigrant cultures of the United States. The contributions these diverse ethnic groups have made and continue to make have a tremendous impact on life in this nation. Our interest in different cultures is often awakened by world events, and libraries should always try to be responsive to these opportunities. The public library must continuously assist in eradicating ignorance and intolerance by integrating cultural diversity into its collections.

Library collections naturally reflect the personal opinions and prejudices of their creators, even the most well-intentioned selectors. This is also true of reviewers and compilers of bibliographies. Selectors must remain cognizant of this subjectivity and always strive to overcome their personal eccentricities as well as the biases inherent in the selection aids they consult. Librarians must ask themselves several questions. Will using only the standard sources result in a sufficient number of multicultural titles or in a core collection written generally for and by white, English-speaking males? Can core collections then be accused of the same narrow-mindedness that was leveled against the editorial board of the Modern Library when it issued its list of best books in 1998? Or even earlier, against the 1959 *Great Books of the Western World*?

An explicit commitment to core collection diversity must be made to compensate for selectors' attitudes. Whenever you are using a recommended bibliography as a core checklist, be cautious that the compilers themselves have considered the importance of cultural diversity in their citations. Careful examination of contributors and the criteria they employed in creating the bibliography can assist this determination. Core selectors may decide on a policy to include titles with fewer citations or "hits" but ones that more closely mirror the ethnic components of the library's users and reflect the cultures of its community. Unfortunately, this is almost a necessity, for there are only a limited number of bibliographies with multicultural titles. Selectors should seek out yearly literary awards given specifically in their state or through an organization that reflects their community's ethnic makeup. For example, the yearly Arizona Book Awards, given to an Arizona author, publisher, or book about our state, are an important source for potential core titles. Also consider the Before Columbus Foundation and its yearly American Book Awards (not to be confused with the National Book Awards, which used the same name from 1980 to 1986). This foundation seeks to recognize contemporary American multicultural literature: "Literary excellence demands a panoramic perspective. A narrow view strictly to the mainstream ignores all tributaries that feed it. American literature is not one tradition but all traditions."[3] Several ethnic sources are included in the chapter 6 list of core selection resources. Librarians may consider developing different criteria for certain multicultural subjects to ensure adequate inclusion of core titles that reflect their community's cultural diversity—an affirmative action plan for core selection.

EQUALITY OF CORE TITLES

It might be assumed that a classic is a classic and that all core titles are created equal. Unfortunately, selection is just not that simple. Choosing core titles emphasizes this difficulty when selectors are deciding among titles that are of high quality but incredibly dissimilar. For example, how does one begin to compare the Old Testament, Homer's *Odyssey*, Shakespeare's *Hamlet*, Charles Darwin's *On the Origin of Species*, Margaret Mitchell's *Gone with the Wind*, John Steinbeck's *Grapes of Wrath*, Toni Morrison's *Beloved*, and Harper Lee's *To Kill a Mockingbird*? You can't! Each of the aforementioned books is a highly acclaimed title, all the novels are Pulitzer Prize winners, and, most important, every one of these titles is still being read. Yet they are so dissimilar they cannot be compared to one another. It would be unreasonable to evaluate all titles using *Macbeth* or the *Iliad* as a benchmark.

Once a selector has discovered that a title has been consistently well reviewed and has received several positive selection criteria "hits," then the title must be judged on its individual merit and suitability for the library and its users. Unfortunately, there is no clear-cut model or hard-and-fast rule to apply in every case to assess whether a title should be included in the core collection. Instead there are general criteria, which are listed in the sample selection statement found in figure 2.1. These can assist selectors in evaluating an individual title. Personal examination or "systematic skimming" (see chapter 3) can further enhance an experienced librarian's core decision making.

Fiction selection presents its own challenges. Often the most lauded of novels is unique and difficult to compare to others. Fiction reviews are totally subjective and based on a reviewer's personal likes and dislikes. It is only by a thorough polling of existing selection media that a librarian can make an informed core decision. Librarians are usually better read in fiction than in nonfiction, and their firsthand knowledge is valuable to the assembly of a fine core list. The more staff involved in core fiction selection, the better the resulting list. A core fiction list is included in chapter 7 to assist libraries in fiction core work. It is certain to provoke discussion and can prove an excellent starting point for core work. Smaller libraries with limited budgets or libraries a bit overwhelmed by the complexity of the core process might initially elect to implement only fiction core collections. This is a good choice because staff knowledge and interest greatly enhance the core process, and core novels are likely to be well received by the library's users. This positive experience will improve the attitude of selectors when they face the nonfiction portion of the collection.

If a library decides to develop genre core collections of science fiction, mystery, western, or romance books, the selection decisions become even more difficult. It is virtually impossible to compare the literary merits of Frank Herbert's *Dune* or Raymond Chandler's *Big Sleep* (both of which are classics of their respective genres) to the novels of Henry James or Willa Cather. Developing good-quality genre collections is, however, very satisfying, because these are titles that are certain to circulate. Again, it is a collection area that staff will be very interested in developing and sharing their opinions. Discussion of genre titles always elicits the most lively of core discussions.

Genre core lists prove helpful in providing readers' advisory assistance to library users, who always appreciate any "what to read next" suggestions. Sample genre core lists can be found in chapter 7 as well. Do not attempt to compare each work of fiction to every other, because this just confuses the entire process. The single most important thing to remember when choosing core novels is to keep the various forms of fiction writing separate in your mind and judge a title's inherent quality only within its separate genre.

Portions of the nonfiction core collection present their own sets of problems. Some subject areas are more difficult to select than others and may warrant developing additional core criteria or soliciting more community experts' advice. Selectors may desire a more detailed listing of a core subject's idiosyncrasies than those listed in the library's collection development policy. If you are selecting core titles in religion, for example, it can be difficult to have basic representation of all the major religions (itself difficult to ascertain) yet steer clear of polemics and political posturing. A library might decide which religions to consider for its core collection on the basis of community demographics. Art books present a different set of problems. The finest and best art books are often prohibitively expensive. Cost coupled with the high theft and mutilation rates means that these books are rarely purchased for branches. A compromise might need to be reached on what quality of core art books the library can afford to include in the collection, perhaps establishing a maximum cost per item before core work commences.

Typically necessary is an agreed-upon list of subject-specific selection aids, book lists, and bibliographies that must be consulted. How this list is accomplished is up to the individual library. Libraries using the committee approach need to have a core committee chairperson who can field the committee's questions as the core work progresses and determine how best to proceed. The core committee chair could also assign which of the additional subject selection aids are to be consulted and by which selector. It is a good idea to submit the additional core criteria and selection sources along with the finalized core selection list. This explains to librarians how the committee's core decisions were made and increases the validity of the finalized core selections. Knowing what additional criteria and core selection resources were utilized is certain to assist library staff in better understanding a subject's core collection parameters.

A library might even decide to skip an entire subject area, whether because there appears to be no community interest or because the library's collections are already so well developed in this subject that core titles are thought to be redundant. Having said this, I must add that I find it unlikely. Perhaps an area is already sufficiently developed and all that needs to be done is to designate appropriate titles as core and label them accordingly. At the Phoenix Public Library, we found that many of our preconceived notions of what would circulate and what our patrons would read were incorrect. Often such notions were based on our personal biases and underestimated the public's interest and thirst for high-quality writing.

Specific nonfiction core criteria might explain, as we discussed earlier, the need for low-water gardening books in Phoenix or additional cookbooks of a particular region or culture that reflect the ethnic makeup of the library's community. The core policy might also specify toward what readership level a subject is to be geared. In the case of medicine, for example, will the core collection contain titles geared only for the educated layperson, or for the health-care professional as well? In core collection development, much like the general collection, the library might decide to collect on different levels for certain subject areas depending on the interests and needs of the library's community.

Core collections do not need to be well balanced and have a representative title for every subject. Core inclusion can be decided on a title-by-title basis, with the provision that the best book available on the subject is being selected. This variation among core subject areas allows libraries that are unable to develop core collections for every subject to choose how much or how little core work needs to be done for their own collection.

ALTERNATE FORMATS OF CORE TITLES

Library collections now include many different formats of materials: films on DVD, audiobooks, music CDs, and e-books are just a few of the formats prevalent today. Decisions need to be made about whether to include these alternate formats as part of a library's core collections. If they are included, will the same selection standards be used to purchase these formats? In the case of audiobooks or e-books, will these formats be purchased as substitutes for the printed book or merely as alternatives? Or will they be considered solely on their own merit? The core collection policy statement should address these questions.

Ideally, if funds and space allow, it would enrich a library's resources to establish film and music core collections as well as an audiobook collection. Films, like music recordings, have their own set of selection aids, yearly awards, and "best of" lists, so both of these core collections could be created following much the same principles as used for the print core collection. Naturally there are differences in an audiovisual selection policy because of the technical issues inherent in these formats. Good nonfiction videos are difficult to find for many subjects, particularly at a reasonable price. A policy decision could be made to buy how-to videos only on those subjects that are better understood by being viewed, much as hearing a language on an audio CD is an essential supplement to learning a language. For example, it is helpful to see how wallpaper is hung, how to cook a chicken, or how to give a massage, but there is no benefit to watching a video on how to write a resume. Whether a library chooses to collect films on DVD is totally dependent on what the library thinks would best serve its users. In chapter 7, a sample feature film core list addresses these issues.

A library must also decide if these alternate formats are to be a substitute for printed books. If a library has an unabridged recording of Nathaniel Hawthorne's *Scarlet Letter* or the latest film version of this classic, for example, does this suffice for the core collection? Is the print copy therefore unnecessary? I certainly hope not, particularly because the 1995 film version changed Hawthorne's tale into one with a happy ending. Demi Moore, who starred as Hester Prynne in this remake, felt the changes to Hawthorne's novel were not a concern because "hardly anybody's read the book." Although this is an unusually blatant desecration of an important literary work, many films based on classics have substantial changes; therefore, it would be difficult to justify using a film to replace the original book or using a novelization of a movie instead of the actual film in the core collection.

I prefer to think that no library would be willing to allow an abridged recording to replace a print copy of a core title. An unabridged recording or an electronic version of a core title might be acceptable as a substitute for the printed book—much as it pains me to say it. Ideally, it would be best if all three formats could be offered, but this depends on a library's budget and available space. If a library does allow an unabridged audiobook to suffice for a core title, there are still standards of technical quality to be met. In the case of an e-book supplanting a printed one, a library should be certain that enough members of the community have ready access to e-book readers or computers.

CORE COLLECTION: FINAL THOUGHTS

Throughout these chapters we see the importance of core collections for today's libraries and an outline of specific steps for creating them. Librarians are the ones who must take the crucial first step and commit to creating a core collection, and then get to work. This is easier than it sounds. There are always reasons not to add yet another project to a librarian's workload, but the importance and benefits of a core collection outweigh the deterrents. If need be, begin with only one subject area.

No doubt there are still librarians who are uncertain whether core collections have a future in today's libraries in light of the vast amounts of digital technology available, all of which is vying for library users' limited time and the library's limited funds. Ironically, designers of video game software do not have these doubts. They are looking to the world's great literature "to deepen and broaden games into a true art form." The *Odyssey* is required reading for electronic arts engineers who are creating video games that will be "famous forever" and that designers have termed "creative storytelling in the digital environment."[4]

President Obama, certainly our most techno-savvy president to date, has often talked about his love of reading and the written word and its ability to "transform": "With the right words everything could change—South Africa, the lives of ghetto kids just a few miles away, my own tenuous place in the world."[5] The reading list of books that shaped his thinking (find it at Amazon and on his Facebook page) contains many likely core titles: Melville's *Moby Dick*, Toni Morrison's *Song of Solomon*, Gandhi's autobiography, Ralph Ellison's *Invisible Man*.

Individual librarians must decide how best to proceed in creating an outstanding core collection. They are the ones who know their library and the community it serves. There are many ways to create a core collection, and selectors should be flexible when designing their own selection procedures. Just remember the four basics of successful core collection development work: (1) a detailed collection policy statement as a buying plan, (2) staff involvement, (3) thorough title assessment, and (4) collection evaluation. And always remember: When in doubt, just leave it out!

After you read this guidebook, it should be clear that no magic formula exists for determining which titles should be in a library's core collection. Mortimer Adler, in his 1940 classic *How to Read a Book*, suggested a simple test that may help a librarian decide which books are truly core and have continuing value for their readers. To take this test, which he claimed was "quite popular a generation ago," you must imagine that "you would know in advance that you will be marooned on a desert island for the rest of your life. . . . You would be allowed ten books. Which are the ones you would select?"[6] It is amusing to note that over seventy years later a form of this test has become wildly popular again, but this time as the Survivor television series. Perhaps this desert island survivor test is a bit simplistic, but it has some validity because books that are classics sustain their importance for readers no matter where they are living or who they are.

In *Living with Books*, Helen Haines warns librarians to be sensitive to the value of fine reading for library users and to be wary of applying selection policies and criteria too heavy-handedly:

All the principles and tests and suggestions that can be formulated may be applied with an insensitivity that renders them useless or a wavering uncertainty that nullifies them. Only by living with books in the spirit as well as in material contact and use, by sharing intellectually and emotionally their many-sided relationship to people and life, does reasoned judgement become instinctive and assured; but such judgement never assumes infallibility. Authority (which is knowledge) and flexibility (which is sympathy) are the two great requirements for bringing to readers the books which are the best for them.[7]

In 1999, the Nobel Lecture was given by Günter Grass, himself a prize winner. He spoke eloquently about the importance of books as a "form of survival as well as a form of art." Grass, who grew up in Nazi Germany, said that he came from the land of book burning and concluded that "our common novel must be continued. And even if one day people stop or are forced to stop writing and publishing, if books are no longer available, there will be storytellers giving us mouth-to-ear artificial respiration, spinning old stories in new ways: loud and soft, heckling and halting, now close to laughter, now on the brink of tears."[8] Let our libraries join in allowing the novel and today's stories to be continued and retained for future generations.

I am hopeful that librarians will continue to "live with books" and develop core collections to ensure that the very best literature continues to be available to library users. Please do not allow libraries to turn into "ghostly data-nodes, characterized less by the breadth of their collections than by the depth of their access."[9] Librarians must remain "core activists" and strive to provide well-stocked libraries for every citizen.

Notes

1. William A. Katz, *Collection Development: The Selection of Materials for Libraries* (New York: Holt, 1980), 94.
2. "USA's Racial, Ethnic Changes Swift in Past Decade," *USA Today*, April 16, 2001, A8.
3. "American Book Awards," http://beforecolumbusfoundation.org.
4. Elizabeth Weise, "The Game's the Thing: Software Designers Look to Great Literature to Turn Fun into a Cultural Force," *USA Today*, April 10, 2001, D1–2.
5. "From Books, New President Found Voice," *New York Times*, January 19, 2009, A1.
6. Mortimer J. Adler and Charles Van Doren, *How to Read a Book*, rev. and updated (New York: Simon and Schuster, 1972), 344.
7. Helen E. Haines, *Living with Books: The Art of Selection*, 2nd ed. (New York: Columbia University Press, 1950), 569.
8. Günter Grass, "To Be Continued . . . ," Nobel Lecture, 1999, http:/nobelprize.org.
9. "Are Bookstores Replacing Libraries," *Utne Reader*, July/August 1993, 32.

CHAPTER 6

CORE SELECTION RESOURCES AND WORKS CITED

The librarian who is not something of an author-
ity on books is, whatever his technical train-
ing, as much out of place as the doctor who
knows nothing of the value of his medicines.
—*New York Libraries,* July 1911

THIS BIBLIOGRAPHY OF CORE selection resources provides a starting point for core collection development. It is by no means an exhaustive list, but it should function as a kind of treasure map for selectors as they begin their quest to locate the best books for their library. The possibilities for locating core titles are endless and clearly illustrate the librarian's ongoing lament: "So many books, so little time." This list can point the way to the types of books and online databases that will assist selectors as they search for core titles. From these cumulative titles, core selectors should be able to build an individualized and unique core collection that is most suited for the particular needs of their library's community.

STANDARD RETROSPECTIVE CORE SELECTION SOURCES

The following titles are important standard sources for retrospective listings of basic books recommended for public libraries. All these selection sources are valuable for locating potential core titles and excellent starting points when beginning the search for core possibilities. Even though several of these books have not been updated recently, they are still viable for core collection development as long as selectors continue to consult other more recent resources. Several of the multivolume sets mentioned below have been updated, and if a library owns these new editions or the online edition that is great. However, considering the steadfastness of core titles and possible budget limitations, it is not necessary for every library to update these expensive sets. Selectors might be lucky enough to pick up an earlier edition for a reduced price, or a set might be theirs for the asking from a library that is discarding them.

Time permitting, every selector should check each of these basic checklists for core candidates, even though entries can be questionable and idiosyncratic. Inclusion in any of the following sources does not mean that a title should definitely be designated as core; rather, exclusion from these sources signals that the title is *not* recommended and, therefore, is most likely not of core caliber. Each librarian must decide individually which titles belong in the library's core collection. When a core title is located in any of these sources, that source should be noted directly on the core list or selection tracking form.

Public Library Core Collection: Fiction (formerly *Fiction Catalog*). 15th ed.
    New York: H. W. Wilson, 2006.
Retrospective source for novels and short stories. This initial volume includes over eight thousand recommended titles that have been selected by librarians from public library systems and will be updated by three annual supplements. Most entries are annotated with an excerpt from a published review with sufficient bibliographic information to lead to the complete review. Out-of-print titles are included and noted as such. Brief publishing history and major awards are given, as is series information. Authors are listed as their names appear on the title page, though cross-references are included for variations of an author's name. The catalog includes a title and subject index that can be useful in answering readers' advisory questions.

Titles are geared to adults, but many are also suitable for high school and academic libraries. H. W. Wilson designates public library systems of varying sizes and geographic locations to participate in the selection of titles for the catalog. Lengthy voting lists are sent to several librarians in one library system. Participants are asked to note whether they think a title should be included in the catalog or to indicate if they are not familiar with the title. Undoubtedly participants are using different selection criteria, for none are given. Although this is a good place to begin a search for core novels, as the catalog's preface states, a title's inclusion is "not an infallible Guide to its quality as literature." This source is also available as an H. W. Wilson electronic database that is updated regularly, and newer titles have expanded review coverage.

Public Library Core Collection: Nonfiction (formerly *Public Library Catalog*).
    13th ed. Edited by John Greenfieldt and Patrice Bartell. New York:
    H. W. Wilson, 2008.
Another H. W. Wilson guide compiled for public libraries and similar in format and execution to the fiction edition. Recommended list of adult reference and nonfiction books for public libraries classified by subject and arranged by Dewey call number. There are yearly supplements, and an updated edition is reissued every five years. Full bibliographic information is given for each title along with a descriptive evaluation from a quoted source. The original edition

lists approximately nine thousand titles, which were chosen by a committee of librarians; an additional three thousand are added through the three annual supplements. There is a helpful author, title, and subject index. Also available as an electronic database, updated regularly; recent titles have expanded reviews.

The Reader's Adviser. 6 vols. 14th ed. Edited by Marion Sader. New
    Providence, N.J.: R. R. Bowker, 1994.
This six-volume guide to the best books for public libraries states that its "aim is to provide the user with a broad and specific view of the great writings and great writers of the past and present." In the present set, the first volume covers the best in reference works and in British and American literature, and volume 2 covers world literature in translation. The third volume is devoted to social sciences, history, and the arts, the fourth to philosophy and world religions, and the fifth to science, technology, and medicine. The sixth volume is a combined index to all volumes. Although this edition has not been updated, it remains an excellent source for core titles and is still available for purchase.

Resources for College Libraries (RCL). 7 vols. Edited by Marcus Elmore.
    Association of College and Research Libraries/R. R. Bowker. 2006.
The long-awaited new edition replacing *Books for College Libraries* (3rd ed.) is a seven-volume listing of recommended "best books" for academic libraries arranged by LC classification and author. Bowker describes this source as a "successor" because of the name change and the fact it is available as an electronic database for the first time. Essentially it is a new edition of the reliable guide of recommended titles for college libraries. Titles were selected by over three hundred teaching faculty and college librarians specifically for undergraduates at a college or small university library. Many of the titles are appropriate for public libraries. *RCL* is also available as an online edition, which is updated quarterly.

Waldhorn, Arthur, Olga S. Weber, and Arthur Zeiger, eds. *Good Reading:*
    A Guide for Serious Readers. 23rd ed. New York: R. R. Bowker, 1990.
This much-respected, fully annotated listing of significant books is arranged in five sections: Historical Periods, Regional and Minority Cultures, Literary Types, Humanities and Social Sciences, and Sciences. Each section includes an explanatory essay written by one of the over thirty contributors, who are, for the most part, subject specialists in university and public libraries. Lists of vacation reading, after-retirement reading, before-college reading, and "101 Significant Books" are also included. This is another excellent Bowker resource that has not been updated; however, its value as a tool for developing a core collection remains unchallenged, and it is still available for purchase.

ADDITIONAL CORE SELECTION RESOURCES

The following titles can be helpful when you are searching for core candidates. This list is meant to be informative but is in no way a complete list of core selection sources. These are general selection aids geared for the educated layperson. Countless subject-specific bibliographies and checklists claim to include only the "best" books, but these must always be approached cautiously to ascertain that the titles are accessible to the educated layperson and that there is sufficient interest on the part of the general library user to warrant inclusion in the core collection. Examples of subject-specific selection resources can be found in chapter 7, where they accompany sample subject core lists. Yearly compilations of "best of" lists can yield core titles; therefore, several of these highly respected lists are included here.

The book club titles listed here all contain lists of recommended titles for reading clubs. Again, these are only guides and not the final word on whether a book should be included in a core collection. The standards of literary merit vary in these lists; however, most are certain to contain some core candidates. Sources with lists of possible core titles are noted with an asterisk (*). Collection development titles providing information on selection policy statements, programming, planning, and publicity can also be found here. Current working selection policies from numerous libraries across the country can be obtained directly through a simple Google or Yahoo! Internet subject search. Additional titles listed here give insight into the philosophy of lifelong reading and the value of great books. I hope these more philosophical books will inspire and motivate selectors as they begin to establish library collections of classics and core titles.

Although some of these sources were published over a decade ago, they, much like the timeless books they describe, are still classics on aspects of collection development and selection and continue to have validity and usefulness for core collection development. In most cases, any of these resources will help create your library's own community-appropriate core collection.

---

*Arozena, Steven, ed. *Best Books for Public Libraries: The 10,000 Top Fiction and Nonfiction Titles.* New Providence, N.J.: R. R. Bowker, 1992.
Designed to give librarians a one-volume guide to the top critically acclaimed books suitable for the general reader. All titles included received positive reviews from at least two of the fifteen commonly consulted book review sources, including many of the review sources listed below.

Birkerts, Sven. *Gutenberg Elegies: The Fate of Reading in an Electronic Age.* Boston: Faber and Faber, 1994.
Disturbing essays that are an indictment of our culture's willingness to embrace new technology at the expense of the printed word.

Books of the Century: A Hundred Years of Authors, Ideas, and Literature. Edited by Charles McGrath and the staff of the Book Review. New York: Times Books, 1998.
Appearing for the first time in book form, more than one hundred years of reviews, essays, interviews on great books and authors of our times; all culled from the pages of the *New York Times Book Review.*

*Boxall, Peter, ed. *1001 Books You Must Read before You Die.* New York: Universe/Rizzoli, 2006.
Yet another entry in the 1001 things that must be accomplished before we die. Despite this much-used title, this is an excellent source for core possibilities. Editor Boxall explains that his use of the number 1001 is actually taken from *The Thousand and One Nights,* the Arabian tales of Sinbad and Aladdin, and their ancient connection between death and storytelling. These 1001 mostly fictional titles were selected by a team of international critics, writers, academics, and journalists. They are arranged by publication date and accompanied by critical, often opinionated, essays that explain why they were included and their relevance today. The reproductions of period dust jackets and book designs that accompany the essays make this book a visual treat.

*Castro, Rafaela G., Edith Maureen Fisher, Terry Hong, and David Williams. *What Do I Read Next? Multicultural Literature.* Detroit: Gale, 1997.
Excellent and unique resource for recommendations to over 1,400 current and classic literature titles from four cultural groups: Asian American, African American, Latino, and Native American. Each of the four authors is an expert on the literature of one of the cultures and compiled the entries as well as the historical overview that begins each section. Each entry lists the age range, subject, time period, and locale of the title along with a summary and other books by the author. Titles from this source are also available in Gale's online database What Do I Read Next? which consolidates the more than 115,000 "recommended" titles from Gale's numerous print series of the same name.

Choice's Outstanding Academic Books, 1992–1997: Reviews of Scholarly Titles That Every Library Should Own. Edited by Rebecca Ann Bartlett. Chicago: Association of College and Research Libraries, 1998.
Respected guide to the best titles for academic libraries. *Choice* magazine's entire review is reprinted for those titles selected as being of the highest overall excellence in presentation and scholarship. The follow-up edition, *Choice's Outstanding Academic Titles, 1998–2002* (the name changed in 2002 to reflect the inclusion of electronic products and Internet sites) is also worth a look. All titles designated as an Outstanding Academic Title (OAT) since 1988 can be found on Choice Reviews Online (www.cro2.org), where they are tagged as such. Many of these titles are also suitable for large public libraries.

*Craughwell, Thomas. *Great Books for Every Book Lover: 2002 Great Reading Suggestions for the Discriminating Bibliophile.* New York: Black Dog and Leventhall, 1998.
The author, who has written each edition of the Book Lover's Page-a-Day calendar since it first appeared in 1995, has put together his personal recommendations. Written in an entertaining style for every type of reader, the book is certain to help you uncover some hidden core gems. Organized by topic, with complete indexes of titles and authors for easy access. Classics in every subject appear with brief informative reviews and complete bibliographic information. Excellent resource for readers' advisory work as well.

Denby, David. *Great Books: My Adventures with Homer, Rousseau, Woolf, and Other Indestructible Writers of the Western World.* New York: Simon and Schuster, 1996.
The film critic of *New York* magazine went back to Columbia University to retake the two required introductory courses in Western classics that he first took in 1961. He recounts his experiences being a student again and rediscovering the powerful lure of great literature. Although not strictly a selection aid, this is an excellent resource for understanding the classics and an excellent introduction to them for the uninitiated.

*Estell, Doug, Michele L. Satchwell, and Patricia S. Wright. *Reading Lists for College-Bound Students.* Stamford, Conn.: Thomson, 2000.
Guide to actual suggested reading lists from over one hundred colleges nationwide. Includes the one hundred works and ten authors most often recommended by colleges and universities along with lists of literary prize winners. Excellent source for mainstream core titles.

*Fadiman, Clifton, and John S. Major. *New Lifetime Reading Plan: Classic Guide to World Literature.* 4th ed. New York: HarperCollins, 1997.
First published over forty years ago, this guidebook now goes beyond the traditional Western canon in selecting its 130 classics. This edition also lists one hundred additional titles written by twentieth-century authors. Detailed bibliography lists other important works and gives suggestions for further reading.

50 Years of Notable Books. Edited by Sandy Whiteley for Booklist Publications. Chicago: American Library Association, Reference and Adult Services Division, 1996.
Every Notable Book for the first fifty years since ALA's Lending Round Table began selecting in 1944 the outstanding books published during the year. The more recent lists can be found on the ALA website. The continuing goal of the list is to encourage people to read books of merit. Important source for core titles.

Gould, Mark, ed. *The Library PR Handbook: High Impact Communications.* Chicago: American Library Association, 2009.
A useful guide to the changing, complex world of library publicity, from print press releases to public service announcements to podcasts.

Guide to Reference Books. 11th ed. Edited by Robert Balay. Chicago: American Library Association, 1996.
Authoritative reference sourcebook with over sixteen thousand annotated entries. This updated edition of the classic Sheehy Guide now includes electronic resources and many more multicultural and ethnic reference sources in addition to titles related to non-European cultures, women's studies, and alternative lifestyles. Although emphasis is on scholarly research, this guide attempts to meet the needs of the practicing public librarian and the general reader. Subject arrangement and extensive indexes make this an excellent source for reference tools to assist you in locating nonfiction core titles. This standard work is now available only as an online subscription and incorporates online reference resources.

*Herald, Diana Tixier, and Wayne A. Wiegand. *Genreflecting: A Guide to Reading Interests.* 6th ed. Englewood, Colo.: Libraries Unlimited, 2005.
Although originally intended as a syllabus for a library school class on reading interests, *Genreflecting* has become an excellent resource for genre authors and titles. Material is divided to define each genre and its subgenres; listed for each genre are annotated bibliographies of suggested titles, best-selling authors, anthologies, history and criticism, book clubs, and publishers.

*Jacobsohn, Rachel W. *The Reading Group Handbook: Everything You Need to Know to Start Your Own Book Club.* Rev. ed. New York: Hyperion, 1998.
A wealth of excellent advice on starting a book club written by a professional reading group leader. Includes over thirty-five reading lists from book clubs all over the country and includes the author's personal recommendations and commentary.

*Kanigel, Robert. *Vintage Reading: From Plato to Bradbury, a Personal Tour of Some of the World's Best Books.* Baltimore: Bancroft, 1998.
Personal guidebook to the world's best books. Author wrote the weekly column "Rereading" for the *Baltimore Sun* and later the *Los Angeles Times* on the joys of rediscovering the world's best literature.

Katz, William A. *Introduction to Reference Work: Basic Information Sources.* Vol. 1. 8th ed. New York: McGraw-Hill, 2001.
This introduction for librarians and library students to the basic sources of reference helps you locate resources to search for core titles in specific subject

areas. Includes basic discussion of the various types of reference works as well as available online sites.

Katz, William A., creator, and Cheryl LaGuardia, editor. *Magazines for Libraries*. 17th ed. New York: R. R. Bowker, 2009.
Over six thousand periodicals listed in subject order, with full text reviews and recommendations. Basically three types of magazines are covered: nonspecialist periodicals written for the layperson, major research journals of distinguished societies, and high-quality commercial publications commonly found in academic and special libraries. This is an excellent standard source for determining the major reviewing magazines in a specific subject area.

*Laskin, David, and Holly Hughes. *The Reading Group Book: The Complete Guide to Starting and Sustaining a Reading Group, with Annotated Lists of 250 Titles for Provocative Discussion*. New York: Dutton Signet, 1995.
A lively, practical guide to reading groups written by two members who belonged to the same book club for fourteen years. The accompanying lists are grouped by subject, such as memoirs, travel, and biography. All include core possibilities.

*Martinez, Sara. *Latino Literature: A Guide to Reading Interests*. Genreflecting Advisory Series. Santa Barbara, Calif.: Libraries Unlimited, 2009.
This useful guide, part of the Genreflecting Advisory Series, focuses on works by Latino authors—U.S. authors of Hispanic heritage and authors from Latin America and Spain. The 750-plus recommended titles are each listed with complete bibliographic information, a short informative plot summary, and award information. This volume, like the others in the series, includes an overview of the genre, a discussion of ethnic terminology, suggestions for selection, publishers, and lists of organization. Other helpful titles in the Genreflecting series include African American literature, Jewish American literature, and World literature. For a complete list, consult Libraries Unlimited's website (http://lu.com).

*Murnighan, Jack. *Beowulf on the Beach: What to Love and What to Skip in Literature's 50 Greatest Hits*. New York: Three Rivers Press, 2009.
An entertaining and irreverent look at fifty classic core titles. The author wants us to get over our guilt about never reading them and realize how great these books really are—a true advocate for core collections.

National Book Awards: Winners and Finalists, 1950–2001. New York: National Book Foundation, 2002.
Listing of the award winners and finalists for the first fifty years of the National Book Awards since they were created in 1950. Visit the National Book Foundation's website (www.nationalbook.org) for the more recent winners.

*National Endowment for the Arts. *The Big Read.* Washington, D.C.:
National Endowment for the Arts, 2008.
This catalog features the books included in the federally funded Big Read
program, which is essentially a community-wide book club. All of these titles
should be considered for any size library's core list. A Big Read program focus-
ing on any one of these books is an excellent way to spotlight your library's core
collection. Grants are awarded by the National Endowment for the Arts yearly.
This booklet and grant applications can be ordered for free or downloaded at
www.NEABigRead.org.

The New Planning for Results: A Streamlined Approach. Edited by Sandra
Nelson for the Public Library Association. Chicago: American Library
Association, 2001.
A classic guide to designing a planning process for public libraries to enable
them to respond to community needs quickly and effectively. Should prove
helpful for librarians as they begin the planning process for core collection
development.

*Parsons, Nicholas. *The Book of Literary Lists.* New York: Facts on File, 1987.
Not all the lists contained in this eccentric collection of literary lists and
anecdotes are helpful in determining core titles, but the creative selector will
find some true gems here along with fanciful groupings of titles that can help
develop unusual book lists.

*Pearl, Nancy. *Book Lust: Recommended Reading for Every Mood, Moment,
and Reason.* Seattle: Sasquatch Books, 2003.

* ———. *More Book Lust: Recommended Reading for Every Mood, Moment,
and Reason.* Seattle: Sasquatch Books, 2005.
Seattle librarian, book reviewer, and lifelong "professional" reader Nancy Pearl
has written two witty and infectious guides to her favorite books. Each contains
about a hundred titles arranged in eclectic groupings. Although this is by no
means a reference guide, the author's personal reading choices, accompanied
by her lively plot summaries including prizes awarded, provide another means
to help you determine a potential title's readability and suitability for core inclusion. Of particular note are the "Not to Be Missed" selections found randomly
throughout these two volumes.

* ———. *Now Read This: A Guide to Mainstream Fiction, 1978–1998.*
Englewood, Colo.: Libraries Unlimited, 1999.

* ———. *Now Read This II: A Guide to Mainstream Fiction, 1990–2001.*
Englewood, Colo.: Libraries Unlimited, 2002.
Each volume of this wonderfully helpful series is an annotated list of one
thousand acclaimed and award-winning novels. Each is selected on the basis

of one of four possible "appeal characteristics": setting, story, characters, and language. A brief annotation for each title describes its strengths, what sets it apart, and secondary appeal characteristics. Each title's subject and additional suggested readings are also given. A two-volume set is available at a reduced rate from Libraries Unlimited, or they can be purchased separately.

The Reader's Catalog: An Annotated Selection of More Than 40,000 of the Best Books in Print in 300 Categories. 2nd ed. Edited by Geoffrey O'Brien et al. New York: New York Reader's Catalog, 1997.
Buying guide that provides access to over forty thousand of the supposedly best books in print divided into fifteen broad categories and over three hundred subcategories. Wonderfully illustrated throughout by the renowned literary caricaturist David Levine, staff artist for the *New York Review of Books*.

Robertson, Deborah A., *Cultural Programming for Libraries: Linking Libraries, Communities, and Culture.* Chicago: American Library Association, 2005.
The director of ALA's Public Programs Office offers a practical and easy-to-use guide that covers all the basics of library programming. Included are helpful discussions of eleven "five-star" outstanding events and samples of promotional materials that can be adapted to develop a core marketing plan.

*Saricks, Joyce G. *Readers' Advisory Guide to Genre Fiction.* 2nd ed. Chicago: American Library Association, 2009.
Good resource with "sure bets" lists that can prove helpful for selecting genre fiction core titles.

*Sleazak, Ellen. *The Book Group Book: A Thoughtful Guide to Forming and Enjoying a Stimulating Book Discussion Group.* 3rd ed. Chicago: Chicago Review, 2000.
Insightful and practical essays about the pragmatic and emotional workings of reading groups of all sizes and orientations. Includes twenty-eight tested reading lists, many annotated.

Ulrich's Periodicals Directory, 2009. 47th ed. New Providence, N.J.: Bowker, 2008.
Premier serials reference source for periodicals. Over 225,000 serials are listed in subject order. Complete bibliographic and access information is given for each periodical, from subscription rates to latest websites, including a brief description of contents and editorial focus. This is an excellent resource for finding specialty magazines on a wide range of subjects of interest to core selectors. Also available as an online version, Ulrichsweb.

REVIEW SOURCES FOR CORE SELECTION

Core titles are normally selected from retrospective selection sources. During core selection, reviews are consulted as a means of determining the suitability of a title discovered in a routine check of a bibliography of recommended titles or a "best of" checklist. Unlike selection for the general collection, where timeliness is important, reviews of potential core titles are usually consulted *after* a title has appeared in a retrospective listing of recommended titles or has received a literary award. Reviews provide additional information on a core candidate and are used to establish whether the work is truly outstanding in its own right and appropriate for library users. On rare occasions a title is published to great critical acclaim and receives such extraordinary reviews that it may be considered for core inclusion the same year it is published. Selectors should read reviews to keep abreast of what is being published and to keep track of well-reviewed titles. Most of the review media listed publish a "best of," "editor's choice," or "summer reading" list of those titles that their staff feel are the exceptional titles for the year. For example, in early December the *New York Times Book Review* includes such a list; *Choice* selects what it calls its "OAT" (Outstanding Academic Titles) annually; *Booklist* and *Library Journal* both publish annual lists of their most recommended titles. Many of the popular magazines, like *Time* and *Newsweek*, also publish their choices for the best books of the year. These lists are always worth examining for core possibilities and help add yet another notch to a selector's list of "hits." Most of these magazines are also available as online subscriptions. Many provide varying degrees of access to their publications at no charge directly through their websites, offering a look at their scope and potential value for your core selection needs.

Booklist. Chicago: American Library Association, since 1905. Bimonthly
    except July and August.
Print and nonprint reviews written for the small to medium-sized public library. Inclusion in the magazine indicates that the title is recommended, so most of the reviews are positive, making it difficult to determine those titles that are exceptional. The starred and highlighted reviews are somewhat helpful and worth a second look, although it is not always clear why they have been singled out. These are short, concise reviews which, on occasion, point out weaknesses even though the title is recommended. Reviews cover all subjects and include nonprint formats such as films, filmstrips, recordings, and software. Foreign-language books and government documents are also listed. Reviews and additional reading lists can also be found online at www.booklistonline.com.

Bookmarks. Chapel Hill, N.C. Bimonthly.
This magazine is for the reading consumer and bills itself as being "for everyone who hasn't read everything." Issued bimonthly, it compiles book reviews for

mostly highly rated titles from many different sources, summarizes them, and then provides a critical review. The magazine keeps an online database of book reviews from the major newspapers and magazines. Its eye-opening year-end chart of the "best of the best" is extremely interesting. You can access this database (www.bookmarksmagazine.com) and see which books are being reviewed currently and how they are faring. An excellent way for core selectors to compare reviews easily and gain familiarity with the different review media.

Choice. Middletown, Conn., Association of College and Research Libraries, since 1963. Eleven issues a year.

About six hundred reviews of recent academic titles geared for academic libraries and written by college professors and academic librarians, many with advanced degrees. Covers titles not found in other review sources. A quarter of the titles reviewed are from university presses. Reviewers are subject specialists and often compare the new title with similar ones previously published, then assign one of five recommendations that appear at the end of each review. Included are monthly selected topics with one or more bibliographic essays. Subscriptions to Choice Reviews Online are available with full review content along with access to the entire database of *Choice* reviews since September 1988. Libraries with subscriptions to either version can also subscribe to Choice Reviews on Cards, which are printed index cards of each individual review that can be useful for sorting and distribution to selectors.

Kirkus Reviews. New York: Kirkus Associates, since 1933. Biweekly.

Long considered the most critical and literary of the library review media. Prepublication reviews with starred reviews of interesting and exceptional titles. Online access to archived reviews since 1933 remains available, but the magazine's future is uncertain.

Library Journal. New York: Reed Elsevier, since 1876. Semimonthly.

Reviews adult books and audiovisuals for public libraries. Quality of reviews can be uneven, since reviewers are well meaning but not paid. Most helpful for core selection are the numerous "best of" lists published throughout the year. Online subscriptions are also available.

New York Review of Books. New York: New York Review, since 1963. Biweekly.

These lengthy intellectual book reviews, often written by well-known authors for the well-educated reader, offer commentary and opinion on politics, literature, science, and culture. Articles from the current issue, plus articles dating back to 1963, and literary podcasts are available online (www.nybooks.com).

New York Times Book Review. New York: New York Times, since 1896. Weekly.

Well-written extended reviews by distinguished authors of noteworthy books. These reviews are often harbingers of a book's future success; a front-page review will most likely result in increased sales and often best-sellerdom. The *Book Review* includes weekly best-seller lists and essays on trends in literature, culture, and publishing. Special compilations of best books are published throughout the year, including recommended summer reading and holiday gift suggestions, all of which are extremely useful for core selection. Although the *Book Review* is a section of the Sunday newspaper, it can be purchased or subscribed to separately.

Publishers Weekly. New York: Reed Elsevier, since 1872. Weekly.
Written for the book trade, reviews are prepublication and concise. Emphasis is placed on a title's salability and potential demand. Books of high interest or special merit are highlighted. Audiobooks are also reviewed. Includes articles on news and trends in the publishing industry. A limited online issue (www.publishersweekly.com) includes some access to the magazine's archives through 1995.

TLS (formerly *Times Literary Supplement*). London: Times Supplements, since 1902. Weekly.
Devoted entirely to well-written reviews, which tend to be lengthy and geared toward the intellectual reader. Although this is a British publication, many reviews are of U.S. titles, offering a different world perspective. Also available as an online subscription with access to the *TLS* archives.

INDEXES TO REVIEWS

Reviews appearing in the magazines listed in the preceding section (along with many others) can be located through the use of general indexes. At present, many of these indexes are available in book or serial format, on CD-ROM, or as online databases. Online subscriptions databases, such as Books in Print, Chadwyck-Healey Title Lists, and Title Source III, often provide full text for their indexed periodicals in addition to numerous other magazines that are merely indexed and abstracted. Whether you use online or print indexes, they allow you to locate reviews of potential core titles quickly. Online databases provide access to many more magazines than do comparable print sources and in recent years have added retrospective titles, making them more helpful for core selection. H. W. Wilson, for example, has expanded its online coverage through its Retrospective Databases Collection, so that many of its indexes such as Book Review Digest now provide complete coverage back to the first print edition. H. W. Wilson also offers subject-specific products such as Social Science Abstracts, General Science Index, and Humanities Abstracts, which provide greater periodical review coverage. For the latest news on these products, check www.hwwilson.com/ftabsind_alpha.htm. Many indexing services are dropping their print editions but have not yet completed retrospective indexing, so you may need to consult both formats, especially for reviews of older titles. Things are changing rapidly online and there are numerous choices now in locating book reviews either in print or online. The same reviews can appear in different indexes; several of the more standard general sources are listed here.

Book Review Digest. New York: H. W. Wilson, since 1905.
Descriptive and critical excerpts from selected reviews of the most popular books published in the United States since 1905 are included from about seventy-five magazines. Includes a helpful subject index to reviews.

Book Review Index. Detroit: Gale, since 1965.
Lists every title that has been reviewed in over three hundred magazines.

Ethnic Newswatch. Ann Arbor, Mich.: Proquest, since 1990.
A unique full-text online source to over three hundred publications that covers ethnic, minority, and American Indian presses. Much of this content is not covered elsewhere.

General Science Full Text Reviews. New York: H. W. Wilson, since 1978.
Starting as a print index in 1978, this online science index covers popular periodicals in the natural sciences, from astronomy to zoology, with a recent emphasis on environmental magazines, as well as medical and physical sciences. Includes articles, reports, and reviews. This index, like other H. W. Wilson indexes, is edited for the general public and for the nonspecialist who desires additional subject coverage beyond those found in *Readers' Guide.* Subject headings are for the nonexpert, and additional descriptive cross-references are provided for ease of use.

Humanities Index. New York: H. W. Wilson, since 1974.
Covers periodicals in the areas of literature and language, religion and theology, folklore, history, performing arts, classical studies, archaeology, and other subjects.

Index to Book Reviews in the Humanities. Williamstown, Mass.: Philip Thomson, since 1960.
Selectively indexes titles by author, including hard-to-find reviews of titles in the fields of architecture, music, drama, and social sciences.

New York Times Index. New York: New York Times, since 1851.
Provides simple access to book reviews from the *New York Times,* which are listed under "Books and Literature." Books are listed by title with author and reviewer information along with day and location of the review. Motion picture review citations are also included.

Readers' Guide to Periodical Literature. Minneapolis: H. W. Wilson, since 1901.
Classic index to the contents of most major magazines. In the print edition a separate section appears in the back of each issue alphabetically listing all reviews that have appeared in any of the magazines indexed by the guide. Coverage emphasizes reviews of popular fiction and books for the general public.

Social Sciences Index. New York: H. W. Wilson, since 1974.
An index for the general library user that analyzes periodicals in anthropology, psychology, sociology, environmental science, economics, and other related subjects.

CRITICISM ON CORE TITLES AND AUTHORS

The timelessness of core titles most likely means that published criticism is available on either the specific title or author or both. Literary criticism differs from book reviews; criticism goes beyond a cursory description of the title and discusses a book's or writer's place in the literature of the subject. There are numerous multivolume sets of criticism. Listed here are some of the standard sources for literary criticism that can be consulted to investigate the importance and historical significance of a core candidate. These sets are straightforward and relatively easy to use; their titles are indicative of what criticism is included. For more detailed information on any of the titles, see either *Guide to Reference Books* or Katz's *Introduction to Reference Work*, cited earlier in this chapter. Many of these resources also offer online subscriptions, such as the Gale Literature Resource Center.

Classic and Medieval Literature Criticism

Contemporary Literary Criticism

Dictionary of Literary Biography

Literature Criticism from 1400 to 1800

Masterplots

Nineteenth-Century Criticism

Survey of Contemporary Literature

Twentieth Century Authors

Twentieth-Century Literary Criticism

REVIEWS ON THE WEB

There are numerous websites for book reviews, but the user must be wary of who has written the review and the stated purpose of the website, both of which can be difficult to ascertain on the Internet. Many sites provide an "about this site" section, which gives a quick overview of a website, its affiliation, and what information you can reasonably expect to find on it. On some sites the reviews may have been taken directly from the magazines listed earlier in this chapter. This site can be helpful because it gathers all the reviews for one title in one location. Remember that most online sites are relatively new and may not provide retrospective reviews as do print resources. Many bookstores, publishers, and authors also have websites on the Internet. The following general websites are worth looking at and may prove useful for locating reviews or additional information about core candidates. Be forewarned that all these sites are constantly changing and are provided here merely as an introduction to literary websites.

Booksellers

Alibris, www.alibris.com. One of the largest online providers of used and out-of-print books. Over ten thousand booksellers list their inventories on Alibris, often with short synopses and customer evaluations.

Amazon, www.amazon.com. The largest online bookstore, with accompanying reviews for most titles, many reprinted from *Library Journal, Publishers Weekly, Booklist,* and the *Washington Post.* Customer reviews, both positive and negative, are also included. Additional information for many titles including tables of contents and author conversations, and even a peek at the first chapter. Also reviews audiobooks, films, music, and Kindle titles.

Barnes and Noble, www.barnesandnoble.com. Barnes and Noble's online store provides reviews, author information, detailed product descriptions, and customer reviews for many titles.

Powell's City of Books, www.powells.com. Billing itself the largest independent new and used bookstore in the world, Powell's Books in Portland, Oregon, has an online store that provides reviews, staff recommendations, and readers' comments. Includes information on audiobooks, DVDs, and e-books.

Book and Author Information

American Booksellers Association, www.bookweb.org. This industry website offers a fairly comprehensive listing of most literary awards, including its own Indie Buzz Book and Quill Awards.

American Library Association, www.ala.org. Site provides *Booklist*'s "Top of the List" selections, Notable Books winners, Outstanding Books for the College Bound, and other lists of award-winning books.

Arts and Letters Daily, www.aldaily.com. This excellent online source for regularly updated literary news and reviews provides links to most news services, major newspapers, book review magazines, journals and magazines, e-zines, and radio news.

Book Report Network, www.bookreporter.com. Reports on literary events with book reviews, in-depth author features, book excerpts, and author-recommended book lists. Short critical reviews of about four hundred words written by unpaid volunteers. Provides a link to the Network's reading group guides.

Bookmarks magazine, www.bookmarksmagazine.com. This website includes book reviews from the past six years and provides links to many of the major book reviews published during the past year along with links to major recommended reading lists.

Bookspot, www.bookspot.com. Provides links to major book award winners, including genre awards.

Bookwire, www.bookwire.com. Bowker's online resource to the book industry includes author interviews, news, and reviews.

Great Books Foundation, www.greatbooks.org.

Lists of Bests, www.listsofbests.com. More than a thousand best-book lists, including the standard book awards along with best-of lists from the BBC, MLA, and *Time*'s "All-Time 100 Novels." An excellent source for core titles.

National Public Radio, www.npr.org.

New York Times, www.nytimes.com. Includes weekday and Sunday book reviews since 1981, along with expanded best-seller lists and yearly Notable Book Lists.

Oprah.com, www.oprah.com. Oprah Winfrey site with news of her book club and selections, reading guides, and recommended titles.

Salon, www.salon.com. Award-winning online magazine focused on cultural and political criticism; founded in 1995 by two former writers from the *San Francisco Examiner.*

Book Publishers

These sites provide reviews of recent releases; award-winning and well-reviewed books are highlighted. Several of these sites also provide reading group guides complete with discussion topics, possible questions, author biographies, bibliographies, and tips on booking an author.

HarperCollins, www.harpercollins.com.

Penguin Books, www.penguingroup.com.

Prentice Hall, www.prenticehall.com.

Random House, www.randomhouse.com. Includes Modern Library's 100 Best Novels and 100 Best Nonfiction of the twentieth century and Freshman Year Reading (www.FreshmanYearReading .com), recommended titles for students entering college.

Simon and Schuster, www.simonandschuster.com.

LITERARY AWARDS

Book awards are an excellent source of core titles. Each award winner and all the nominated titles for the literary prizes listed should be seriously considered for the core collection. Prestigious awards other than those listed here are given in specific-subject areas, such as the James Beard Foundation Book Award for the year's outstanding cookbooks. These should be included in the subject-specific criteria developed by the individual subject core committees to aid their members' search for core titles. Many of these awards have their own websites, and complete lists of winners can be obtained on the Internet; www.ala.org, www.amazon.com, www.bookspot.com, www.bookwire.com, and www.salon.com are some of the websites that provide portals to many of the awards listed here.

American Library Association Notable Books are chosen annually by the Notable Books Council on the basis of the following criteria: the book has exceptional literary quality; it expands the horizons of human knowledge; it makes specialized knowledge accessible to the nonspecialist; and it promises to contribute to the solution of a contemporary problem.

Book Sense Book of the Year (formerly the ABBY) was created in 1991 by the American Booksellers Association. The purpose was to find a literary gem that ABA bookstore members most enjoyed recommending to their customers during the previous year. Four Book Sense Honor books were also designated. In 2009 this award was replaced by the Indie Choice Awards, which have a distinct public relations bias: Best Indie Buzz Book, Best Conversation Starter, Most Engaging Author. These new awards unfortunately do not provide much help for selections of core titles, but the earlier Book Sense titles are worth considering.

The Booker Prize, also known as the Man Booker Prize, is awarded to the best full-length novel in English by a citizen of the United Kingdom, the Commonwealth of Nations, South Africa, or Pakistan. It is the United Kingdom's most prestigious award. In 2002 a second award for literary excellence was created, the Man Booker International Prize, given every other year to an author of any nationality whose work is available in English.

The Costa Book Awards, until 2006 called the Whitbread Book Awards, are given to the most enjoyable books of the year written by writers based in the United Kingdom and Ireland. Literary excellence is awarded in four adult categories: best novel, first novel, biography, and poetry.

The Kiriyama Pacific Rim Book Prize is given to the book that best promotes an understanding of the peoples and nations of the Pacific Rim. Cosponsored by the Kiriyama Pacific Rim Foundation and the University of San Francisco. At this time the award is being restructured and not accepting entries; past winners are listed on the website (www.kiriyamaprize.org).

The Miles Franklin Award has been given annually since 1957 to the Australian novel or play of the highest literary merit dealing with Australian life.

The National Book Award was created by U.S. publishers. Its juries are composed of writers, critics, and scholars. Awards are given to honor U.S. fiction, nonfiction, and poetry of the highest literary merit. The complete list of nominated titles is announced before the awards.

The National Book Critics' Circle Awards were founded in 1974 and are sponsored and judged by professional book review editors and critics. Awards are given in six categories: fiction, general nonfiction, autobiography, biography, poetry, and criticism.

The National Humanities Medal is awarded by the president of the United States to those who have increased public awareness of the humanities.

The National Medal of the Arts is bestowed by the president of the United States on an individual for outstanding contributions to the arts. This is not always a writer, and the medal has been given to musicians, actors, and painters. The winners, such as architect Frank Gehry, rock and roller "Fats" Domino, and actor Gregory Peck, can signal to the core selector the importance of an individual, which can assist in the selection of films or music as well as books.

The Nobel Prize for literature, first awarded 1901, is chosen by the Swedish Academy as instructed by Alfred Nobel in his will. The prize is awarded in recognition of a body of work rather than an individual title.

The PEN/Faulkner Award was created in 1980 by writers to honor their peers for works of U.S. fiction and is awarded annually by the PEN/Faulkner Foundation. It is named in honor of William Faulkner, who used his Nobel Prize money to establish an award for young writers.

The Prix Goncourt is awarded by writers for outstanding French writing through the Sociéte littéraire des Goncourt.

The Pulitzer Prize is named in honor of the Hungarian-born U.S. newspaper publisher Joseph Pulitzer. Yearly prizes are given for the best books in fiction, nonfiction, poetry, biography, drama, and history. The Pulitzers have been awarded by the trustees of Columbia University since 1917 on the recommendations of an advisory board.

The Stephen Crane 1st Fiction Award was created in 1995 by the Book of the Month Club to honor the most promising literary debut of the year. Nominees are announced before the award.

WORKS CITED

Listed here are the titles most useful to me as I wrote *Developing an Outstanding Core Collection*. This is by no means a definitive list of all the works I consulted. It is intended as an aid for librarians who wish to pursue the ideas put forth here. I have also listed a few titles not cited in the text that had an impact on the writing of this guide and should provide additional core selection guidance. Those titles with an asterisk (*) contain recommended reading lists that might prove helpful as you seek core possibilities.

*Adler, Mortimer J., and Charles Van Doren. *How to Read a Book.* Rev. and
updated. New York: Simon and Schuster, 1972.
Illuminating handbook provides guidance for the general reader on the varying dimensions of reading comprehension. Includes a reading list of what these two scholars think are the "great books"—the ones they feel anyone should choose to take to a desert island. The titles appearing on this list, though somewhat esoteric, should be considered for core collection inclusion.

Anderson, Joanne S., ed. *Guide for Written Collection Policy Statements.*
2nd ed. Collection Management and Development Guides, No. 7.
Chicago: American Library Association, 1996.
Second edition of a highly useful guide that provides step-by-step instructions for the writing of collection development statements for every size library. Includes extensive bibliography for additional reading.

*Beam, Alex. *A Great Idea at the Time: The Rise, Fall, and Curious Afterlife
of the Great Books.* New York: PublicAffairs, 2008.
The *Boston Globe* columnist takes a sharp look at the Great Books mania of the 1940s through '60s when over a million Americans bought these "faux leather sets with unreadable type" of the most quoted, least-read books of our time written by seventy-four "dead, white male authors." For librarians, this can be read as a cautionary tale of exactly what we *do not* want our library's core collections to be. Still the list, updated in 1990 to include Jane Austen and George Eliot, of "The (Randomly Annotated) Great Books of the Western World" at the end of the book is worth examining.

*Bloom, Harold. *How to Read and Why.* New York: Scribner, 2000.
An elegant and witty guide by the renowned literary critic pays tribute to the pleasures and benefits of reading the best literature. The titles included in Bloom's discussions are significant works worth considering for core collections.

Bryant, Bonita, ed. *Guide for Written Collection Policy Statements.*
Collection Management and Development Guides, No. 3. Chicago:
American Library Association, 1989.
First edition of the now standard guide to writing library selection policy statements. This earlier edition provides some clarification of terms and additional steps in the policy statement writing process that are missing in the later edition. Includes an excellent bibliography.

Calvino, Italo. *Why Read the Classics?* Translated by Martin McLaughlin. New York: Pantheon, 1999.
Impassioned philosophical discussion on the enduring importance of reading the Western world's eminent writers.

Cassell, Kay Ann, and Elizabeth Futas. *Developing Public Library Collections, Policies, and Procedures.* How-to-Do-It Manuals for Libraries 12. New York: Neal-Schuman, 1991.
A straightforward how-to manual on collection development written for small and medium-sized public libraries. Covers the steps to creating a collection development policy along with the details of the planning process. Includes a sample collection development statement and an annotated list of selection aids.

Delbanco, Andrew. *Required Reading: Why Our American Classics Matter Now.* New York: Farrar, Straus and Giroux, 1997.
Collection of criticism that explains this nation's common heritage and why our classics are indispensable to an understanding of our society.

*Diefendorf, Elizabeth, ed. *New York Public Library's Books of the Century.* New York: Oxford University Press, 1996.
Compilation of 150 important works selected by the librarians of the New York Public Library in honor of the library's centennial. An explanation of each title's significance and additional readings are provided.

Evans, G. Edward. *Developing Library and Information Center Collections.* 2nd ed. Littleton, Colo.: Libraries Unlimited, 1987.
Practical collection development textbook. Useful as a starting point to an understanding of the many processes of materials selection. Includes a good historical overview on the issues surrounding collection development and the numerous steps necessary for designing a selection process. Provides additional readings at the end of each chapter. Its usefulness, however, is somewhat limited by its publication date, particularly when dealing with serials and the challenges of electronic resources and the Internet.

Fales, Susan L., ed. *Guide for Training Collection Development Librarians.* Collection Management and Development Guides, No. 8. Chicago: American Library Association, 1996.
Helpful guide to assist librarians develop training programs for selectors on the basis of required competencies and sample activities. Includes a lengthy bibliography of resources on collection development and management.

Futas, Elizabeth, ed. *Collection Development Policies and Procedures.* 3rd ed. Phoenix, Ariz.: Oryx, 1995.
An extremely useful compilation of collection development policies. Contains four full statements and excerpts from numerous other libraries' policies

grouped together by similar components for ease of use. Concludes with the ALA's statements on literary freedoms.

Gleick, James. *Faster: The Acceleration of Just about Everything.* New York: Pantheon, 1999.
Brilliantly reasoned and engaging study of our universal obsession with time.

Haines, Helen E. *Living with Books: The Art of Book Selection.* 2nd ed. New York: Columbia University Press, 1950.
The classic work on collection development and selection. Although the material is dated in parts, the author's eloquence and love of books and reading make it worthwhile. Of particular interest are her philosophy of library collection building and her assumption that people need materials for "deeper life channels." A core title in the library science field.

*Hirsch, E. D., Jr. *Cultural Literacy: What Every American Needs to Know.* Boston: Houghton Mifflin, 1987.
This controversial national best-seller asserted that an understanding of common background information is essential for success in America. Contains the "thinking American's lists" of the knowledge the author claims that most literate Americans share. This list can assist with core title selection.

Karp, Rashelle S., ed. *Part-Time Public Relations with Full-Time Results: A PR Primer for Libraries.* Chicago: American Library Association, 2002.
Indispensable guide to the practicalities of library public relations for busy librarians. Samples of press releases and public service announcements are some of the real-life solutions that are presented.

Katz, William A. *Collection Development: The Selection of Materials for Libraries.* New York: Holt, 1980.
The basic principles of collection development, including nonbook formats. This classic covers selection, evaluation, maintenance, and censorship issues as well as practical advice on the acquisition of materials. Another classic in the library field.

*Knight, Brenda. *Women Who Love Books Too Much: Bibliophiles, Bluestockings, and Prolific Pens from the Algonquin Hotel to the Ya-Ya Sisterhood.* Berkeley, Calif.: Conari, 2000.
Witty and charming look at ravenous women readers through the ages. Includes a resource guide for book clubs.

Lockett, Barbara. *Guide to the Evaluation of Library Collections.* Collection Management and Development Guides, No. 2. Chicago: American Library Association, 1989.
This excellent handbook is designed to identify common methods of collection evaluation and includes an extensive bibliography on collection evaluation.

*McMains, Victoria Golden. *The Readers' Choice: 200 Book Club Favorites.* New York: HarperCollins, 2000.
The top reading recommendations of more than seventy book groups nationwide. Page-long profiles highlight the special features of each of the two hundred selections. Includes questions for book discussions. Index is arranged by subject as well as title. Good checklist for core possibilities.

National Endowment for the Arts. *Reading on the Rise: A New Chapter in American Literacy.* Washington, D.C., National Endowment for the Arts, 2009.

———. *To Read or Not to Read: A Question of National Consequence.* Executive Summary. Washington, D.C., National Endowment for the Arts, 2007.

———. *Reading at Risk: A Survey of Literary Reading in America.* Executive Summary. Washington, D.C., National Endowment for the Arts, 2004.
These three reports track the reading habits of adults in the United States over the past five years. In 2009, for the first time in over twenty-five years, the NEA survey showed an increase in "literary" reading, which refers to novels, short stories, poems, or plays read in print or online. Certainly any librarian will find these results exhilarating. Together they are useful documents for promoting core collection development. They can be ordered free online or downloaded at www.arts.gov.

O'Brien, Geoffrey. *The Browser's Ecstasy: A Meditation on Reading.* Washington, D.C.: Counterpoint, 2000.
Novelist and critic and editor of *The Reader's Catalog* takes an unusual look at the joys of browsing through many books at the same time and making connections between them. Of interest to librarians who are continuously browsing through books and attempting to base selection decisions on these mere snippets of writing.

Ryback, Timothy W. *Hitler's Private Library: The Books That Shaped His Life.* New York: Knopf, 2008.
A provocative look at Hitler's personal library and his intellectual life. That the man who burned books had a personal collection of over 16,000 volumes, was a voracious reader, and ranked *Don Quixote, Uncle Tom's Cabin, Gulliver's*

Travels, and Shakespeare as among the world's great literature is eye-opening. *Hitler's Private Library* gives us much to contemplate about the power of the written word and may provoke an interesting book discussion group meeting.

*Shwartz, Ronald B., ed. *For the Love of Books: 115 Celebrated Writers on the Books They Love Most.* New York: Grosset/Putnam, 1999.
Idiosyncratic discussion of books that these contemporary writers have found most impressive. The accompanying bibliography is worth checking for core titles. The essays by these distinguished authors are laden with excellent evaluation techniques and criteria for choosing the "best" books.

*Trounstine, Jean R., and Robert P. Waxler. *Finding a Voice: The Practice of Changing Lives through Literature.* Ann Arbor, Mich.: University of Michigan Press/ESL, 2005.
This volume and the earlier *Changing Lives through Literature* (University of Notre Dame Press, 1999) are inspirational examinations of an alternative sentencing program that has encouraged criminal offenders since 1991 to examine their lives through literature. The authors insist that "literature can make a difference," demonstrate the transformative powers of the CLTL program, and discuss their reading choices, many of them core titles.

CHAPTER 7

SAMPLE CORE LISTS WITH SELECTION CRITERIA AND SOURCES

When in doubt, just leave it out!
—First Law of Core Selection, Phoenix Public Library

IN THIS CHAPTER YOU will find examples of core lists that selectors can adapt to their library's unique core needs or use as a quick and easy way to jump-start a library's core collection. Each of the core list models begins with a brief overview of the subject, including any specific criteria that are unique to it. Special reference sources that were consulted to create the core lists (beyond those listed in chapter 6) are also given. In some cases these are arbitrary and might not work for all libraries. They are included merely as a frame of reference and as examples of how selectors might further define a subject. The criteria and specific sources that will be used to create subject core lists should logically be determined by the core subject committee before selectors begin core work. It should be understood that any additional criteria developed for specific subjects must be considered in conjunction with the sample core collection development policy statement that appears in chapter 2. Those in my hypothetical examples go hand in hand with the Southwest Public Library policy statement in figure 2.1.

Although it is understood that title classifications can vary tremendously from one library to the next, sample nonfiction lists are arranged in rough Dewey call number order, since this is most likely the way core selectors would approach a specific subject. Because cataloging can be arbitrary at times, this may result in a title appearing where it is not expected or not appearing at all because of its call number. These core lists are given as examples only and will need to be fine-tuned to each library's classification idiosyncrasies.

The biography core list is arranged in alphabetical order by the person who is the subject of the book. The fiction core lists are arranged in alphabetical order by the author's name as it appears on the title page. The film core list is in alphabetical order by the movie's title. No attempt has been made to include a specific publisher, edition, or price. Many titles are available in several editions as well as in paperback and hardcover, audiobook, or e-book. The decision of what edition to purchase should be made by the individual selectors, again based on the library's individual needs. A philosophy list has been included because this subject's high use most surprised the librarians throughout the Phoenix Public Library system. This was an area that had never previously been developed to any degree in the branch libraries.

Every attempt has been made to select the best titles using the principles outlined in this book. Although many of the titles listed here were selected by the valiant and excellent core selectors of the Phoenix Public Library along with input from local experts in the community, all the lists have been adapted for this book. All the core lists were developed specifically for this book as sample lists; no one list was created for any specific existing library.

The core criteria and selection sources that accompany each core list were also created specifically for this book, purely to illustrate the principles outlined in earlier pages. Bear in mind that there is no definite answer to exactly what constitutes a core title; selector judgment and experience are the keys. It is my hope that these sample core lists and the accompanying criteria and source material spark debate among library selectors and enable them to mold the lists into viable core collections that fit the needs of their library's community.

SAMPLE FICTION CORE LIST
Criteria and Sources

The following core fiction criteria were developed by the fiction core committee and should be considered in conjunction with the general core criteria as outlined in the Southwest Public Library's core collection development policy statement [see chapter 2]:

1 | No more than three titles by an author.

2 | Titles published within the past five years only if they or their authors have won or been a finalist for at least one of the following major literary awards [see award descriptions in chapter 6].

- Book Sense Book of the Year
- Costa Book Award
- Man Booker Prize
- National Book Award
- National Book Critics' Circle Award
- National Humanities Medal
- National Medal of the Arts
- Nobel Prize

- PEN/Faulkner Award
- Pulitzer Prize
- Stephen Crane 1st Fiction Award

3 | Titles published within the past ten years that have been finalists for a major award may be considered only if (a) the majority of the fiction core committee members who have read the book are in agreement that the title is well written and is of outstanding and lasting merit; (b) the title has at least two excellent reviews by the country's leading critics; and (c) the title appears in at least three of the following excellent bibliographies [for full citations and annotations of some of these sources, see chapter 6].

- *Best Books for Public Libraries*
- Big Read titles
- *Books of the Century: A Hundred Years of Authors, Ideas, and Literature*
- *50 Years of Notable Books*
- *Good Reading*
- *Great Books of the Western World*
- Modern Library's 100 Best Novels and Modern Library's 100 Best Nonfiction
- *New York Public Library's Books of the Century*
- *Now Read This* and *Now Read This II*
- *Outstanding Books for the College Bound*
- *The Reader's Adviser*
- *Reading Lists for College-Bound Students*
- *Time* magazine's All-Time 100 Novels

4 | Although you will undoubtedly use *Public Library Core Collection: Fiction* (formerly *Fiction Catalog*) and reviews in *Publishers Weekly, Library Journal, Booklist,* and *Kirkus* in the search for core fiction titles, none of these is sufficiently selective to fulfill the recommended requirements for core inclusion.

5 | All core forum attendees are to follow these same criteria in recommending fiction titles for the core collection.

Fiction Core List

Abbey, Edward. *The Monkey Wrench Gang.*

Abe, Kobo. *The Woman in the Dunes.*

Achebe, Chinua. *Things Fall Apart.*

Adams, Henry. *Democracy.*

Adams, Richard. *Watership Down.*

Agee, James. *A Death in the Family.*

Agnon, Shumel Yosef. *The Bridal Canopy.*

Algren, Nelson. *The Man with the Golden Arm.*

Allende, Isabel. *The House of the Spirits.*

Amado, Jorge. *Dona Flor and Her Two Husbands.*

Anaya, Rudolfo A. *Bless Me, Ultima.*

Anderson, Sherwood. *Winesburg, Ohio.*

Appelfeld, Aharon. *Badenheim 1939.*

Arnow, Harriette. *The Dollmaker.*

Asch, Sholem. *The Nazarene.*

Atwood, Margaret. *The Blind Assassin.*

Auchincloss, Louis. *The Rector of Justin.*

Austen, Jane. *Emma.*

Austen, Jane. *Pride and Prejudice.*

Austen, Jane. *Sense and Sensibility.*

Baldwin, James. *Giovanni's Room.*

Baldwin, James. *Go Tell It on the Mountain.*

Balzac, Honoré de. *Cousin Bette.*

Barrett, Andrea. *Ship Fever.*

Barth, John. *The Sot-Weed Factor.*

Bellow, Saul. *Humboldt's Gift.*

Bellow, Saul. *Seize the Day.*

Berger, Thomas. *Little Big Man.*

Blasco Ibáñez, Vicente. *The Four Horsemen of the Apocalypse.*

Boll, Heinrich. *Group Portrait with Lady.*

Bowen, Elizabeth. *The Death of the Heart.*

Boyle, T. Coraghessan. *World's End.*

Brontë, Charlotte. *Jane Eyre.*

Brontë, Emily. *Wuthering Heights.*

Brown, Rita Mae. *Rubyfruit Jungle.*

Buck, Pearl. *The Good Earth.*

Bunyan, John. *The Pilgrim's Progress.*

Burgess, Anthony. *A Clockwork Orange.*

Burroughs, William. *The Naked Lunch.*

Butler, Samuel. *The Way of All Flesh.*

Byatt, A. S. *Possession.*

Caldwell, Erskine. *Tobacco Road.*

Camus, Albert. *The Plague.*

Camus, Albert. *The Stranger.*

Capote, Truman. *Breakfast at Tiffany's.*

Carver, Raymond. *Cathedral.*

Cather, Willa. *Death Comes for the Archbishop.*

Cather, Willa. *My Antonia.*

Cervantes, Miguel de. *Don Quixote.*

Chabon, Michael. *The Amazing Adventures of Kavalier and Clay.*

Cheever, John. *The Stories of John Cheever.*

Cheever, John. *The Wapshot Chronicle.*

Chekhov, Anton. *Short Stories.*

Chopin, Kate. *The Awakening.*

Clark, Walter V. *The Ox-Bow Incident.*

Clavell, James. *Shōgun.*

Coetzee, J. M. *Disgrace.*

Colette. *Collected Stories.*
Collins, Wilkie. *The Moonstone.*
Connell, Evan. *Mr. Bridge.*
Connell, Evan. *Mrs. Bridge.*
Conrad, Joseph. *Heart of Darkness.*
Conrad, Joseph. *Lord Jim.*
Conroy, Pat. *The Prince of Tides.*
Cooper, James Fenimore. *Leatherstocking Tales.*
Crane, Stephen. *The Red Badge of Courage.*
Cunningham, Michael. *The Hours.*
Defoe, Daniel. *Moll Flanders.*
Del Vecchio, John M. *The 13th Valley.*
DeLillo, Don. *White Noise.*
Díaz, Junot. *The Brief Wondrous Life of Oscar Wao.*
Dickens, Charles. *David Copperfield.*
Dickens, Charles. *Great Expectations.*
Dickens, Charles. *A Tale of Two Cities.*
Dickey, James. *Deliverance.*
Doctorow, E. L. *Ragtime.*
Doerr, Harriet. *Stones for Ibarra.*
Donoso, Jose. *The Obscene Bird of Night.*
Dos Passos, John. *U.S.A.*
Dostoevsky, Fyodor. *The Brothers Karamazov.*
Dostoevsky, Fyodor. *Crime and Punishment.*
Dreiser, Theodore. *An American Tragedy.*
Dreiser, Theodore. *Sister Carrie.*
Dumas, Alexandre. *The Three Musketeers.*
DuMaurier, Daphne. *Rebecca.*
Eco, Umberto. *The Name of the Rose.*
Eliot, George. *Middlemarch.*
Eliot, George. *The Mill on the Floss.*

Eliot, George. *Silas Marner.*
Ellison, Ralph. *Invisible Man.*
Emecheta, Buchi. *The Bride Price.*
Endo, Shusako. *Silence.*
Erdrich, Louise. *Love Medicine.*
Faulkner, William. *As I Lay Dying.*
Faulkner, William. *The Sound and the Fury.*
Ferber, Edna. *So Big.*
Fielding, Henry. *Tom Jones.*
Fitzgerald, F. Scott. *The Great Gatsby.*
Fitzgerald, F. Scott. *Tender Is the Night.*
Flaubert, Gustave. *Madame Bovary.*
Ford, Richard. *Independence Day.*
Forster, E. M. *A Passage to India.*
Fowles, John. *The French Lieutenant's Woman.*
Fowles, John. *The Magus.*
Frazier, Charles. *Cold Mountain.*
French, Marilyn. *The Women's Room.*
Fuentes, Carlos. *The Death of Artemio Cruz.*
Gaines, Ernest. *The Autobiography of Miss Jane Pittman.*
Galsworthy, John. *The Forsyte Saga.*
García Márquez, Gabriel. *One Hundred Years of Solitude.*
Gilman, Charlotte P. *The Yellow Wallpaper.*
Golding, William. *The Lord of the Flies.*
Goldsmith, Oliver. *The Vicar of Wakefield.*
Gordimer, Nadine. *July's People.*
Grass, Günter. *The Tin Drum.*
Graves, Robert. *I, Claudius.*
Greenberg, Joanne. *I Never Promised You a Rose Garden.*
Greene, Graham. *The Heart of the Matter.*

Guterson, David. *Snow Falling on Cedars.*

Guthrie, Alfred B. *The Big Sky.*

Ha Jin. *Waiting.*

Hardy, Thomas. *Far from the Madding Crowd.*

Hardy, Thomas. *The Return of the Native.*

Hardy, Thomas. *Tess of the D'Urbervilles.*

Hawthorne, Nathaniel. *The House of the Seven Gables.*

Hawthorne, Nathaniel. *The Scarlet Letter.*

Heller, Joseph. *Catch-22.*

Hemingway, Ernest. *A Farewell to Arms.*

Hemingway, Ernest. *For Whom the Bell Tolls.*

Hemingway, Ernest. *The Old Man and the Sea.*

Hersey, John R. *A Bell for Adano.*

Hesse, Herman. *Siddhartha.*

Hesse, Herman. *Steppenwolf.*

Hijuelos, Oscar. *The Mambo Kings Play Songs of Love.*

Hilton, James. *Lost Horizon.*

Hugo, Victor. *The Hunchback of Notre Dame.*

Hugo, Victor. *Les Miserables.*

Hurston, Zora Neale. *Their Eyes Were Watching God.*

Huxley, Aldous. *Brave New World.*

Ishiguro, Kazuo. *The Remains of the Day.*

James, Henry. *The Ambassadors.*

James, Henry. *The Golden Bowl.*

James, Henry. *The Portrait of a Lady.*

Jones, Edward P. *The Known World.*

Jones, James. *From Here to Eternity.*

Jong, Erica. *Fear of Flying.*

Joyce, James. *A Portrait of the Artist as a Young Man.*

Joyce, James. *Ulysses.*

Kafka, Franz. *Metamorphosis.*

Kawabata, Yasunari. *Snow Country.*

Keneally, Thomas. *Schindler's List.*

Kennedy, William. *Ironweed.*

Kerouac, Jack. *On the Road.*

Kesey, Ken. *One Flew over the Cuckoo's Nest.*

Keyes, Daniel. *Flowers for Algernon.*

Kincaid, Jamaica. *Autobiography of My Mother.*

King, Stephen. *The Stand.*

Kingsolver, Barbara. *The Poisonwood Bible.*

Kipling, Rudyard. *Kim.*

Kneale, Matthew. *The English Passengers.*

Knowles, John. *A Separate Peace.*

La Farge, Oliver. *Laughing Boy.*

Lahiri, Jhumpa. *Interpreter of Maladies.*

Lawrence, D. H. *Lady Chatterley's Lover.*

Lawrence, D. H. *Women in Love.*

Lee, Harper. *To Kill a Mockingbird.*

Lethem, Jonathan. *Motherless Brooklyn.*

Lewis, Sinclair. *Main Street.*

Llewellyn, Richard. *How Green Was My Valley.*

London, Jack. *The Call of the Wild.*

Mahfouz, Naguib. *Palace Walk.*

Mailer, Norman. *The Executioner's Song.*

Mailer, Norman. *The Naked and the Dead.*

Malamud, Bernard. *The Assistant.*

Malamud, Bernard. *The Fixer.*

Mann, Thomas. *Death in Venice.*

Mann, Thomas. *The Magic Mountain.*

Marshall, Paule. *Brown Girl, Brownstones.*

Matthiessen, Peter. *At Play in the Fields of the Lord.*

Maugham, W. Somerset. *Of Human Bondage.*

Maupassant, Guy de. *Short Stories.*

McCarthy, Cormac. *All the Pretty Horses.*

McCullers, Carson. *The Heart Is a Lonely Hunter.*

McCullers, Carson. *A Member of the Wedding.*

McCullough, Colleen. *The Thorn Birds.*

McDermott, Alice. *Charming Billy.*

McMurtry, Larry. *Lonesome Dove.*

Melville, Herman. *Billy Budd.*

Melville, Herman. *Moby Dick.*

Michener, James. *Chesapeake.*

Michener, James. *The Source.*

Miller, Henry. *Tropic of Cancer.*

Mishima, Yukio. *Spring Snow.*

Mitchell, Margaret. *Gone with the Wind.*

Momaday, N. Scott. *House Made of Dawn.*

Morrison, Toni. *Beloved.*

Morrison, Toni. *Song of Solomon.*

Murasaki, Lady. *The Tale of Genji.*

Murdoch, Iris. *The Sea, the Sea.*

Nabokov, Vladimir. *Lolita.*

Naipaul, V. S. *A House for Mr. Biswas.*

Nichols, John T. *The Milagro Beanfield War.*

Nordhoff, Charles, and James Norman Hall. *Mutiny on the Bounty.*

Oates, Joyce Carol. *Them.*

O'Brien, Tim. *Going after Cacciato.*

O'Connor, Edwin. *The Last Hurrah.*

O'Connor, Flannery. *Complete Stories.*

O'Hara, John. *Ten North Frederick.*

O. Henry. *Best Short Stories.*

Ondaatje, Michael. *The English Patient.*

Orczy, Emmuska. *The Scarlet Pimpernel.*

Orwell, George. *Animal Farm.*

Orwell, George. *1984.*

Parks, Gordon. *The Learning Tree.*

Pasternak, Boris. *Doctor Zhivago.*

Paton, Alan. *Cry, the Beloved Country.*

Percy, Walker. *The Moviegoer.*

Plath, Sylvia. *The Bell Jar.*

Porter, Katherine Anne. *Collected Stories.*

Potok, Chaim. *The Chosen.*

Proulx, E. Annie. *The Shipping News.*

Proust, Marcel. *Remembrance of Things Past.*

Puig, Manual. *Kiss of the Spider Woman.*

Puzo, Mario. *The Godfather.*

Pynchon, Thomas. *Gravity's Rainbow.*

Rand, Ayn. *Atlas Shrugged.*

Rand, Ayn. *The Fountainhead.*

Remarque, Erich. *All Quiet on the Western Front.*

Rhys, Jean. *Wide Sargasso Sea.*

Rice, Anne. *Interview with the Vampire.*

Richter, Conrad. *The Light in the Forest.*

Robbins, Tim. *Even Cowgirls Get the Blues.*

Robinson, Marilynne. *Gilead.*

Rolvaag, Ole. *Giants in the Earth.*

Roth, Philip. *American Pastoral.*

Roth, Philip. *The Human Stain.*

Roy, Arundhati. *The God of Small Things*.

Rushdie, Salman. *Midnight's Children*.

Salinger, J. D. *The Catcher in the Rye*.

Salinger, J. D. *Franny and Zooey*.

Sanchez, Thomas. *Rabbit Boss*.

Saramago, Jose. *The Gospel according to Jesus*.

Saroyan, William. *The Human Comedy*.

Schwarz-Bart, Andre. *The Last of the Just*.

Scott, Paul. *The Raj Quartet*.

Scott, Sir Walter. *Ivanhoe*.

Shaara, Michael. *The Killer Angels*.

Shelley, Mary. *Frankenstein*.

Shields, Carol. *The Stone Diaries*.

Sholem Aleichem. *Favorite Stories*.

Sholokhov, Mikhail. *And Quiet Flows the Don*.

Shute, Nevil. *On the Beach*.

Sienkiewicz, Henryk. *Quo Vadis*.

Silko, Leslie. *Ceremony*.

Sinclair, Upton. *The Jungle*.

Singer, Isaac Bashevis. *Collected Stories*.

Smiley, Jane. *A Thousand Acres*.

Smith, Betty. *A Tree Grows in Brooklyn*.

Smith, Zadie. *White Teeth*.

Solzhenitsyn, Alexander. *Cancer Ward*.

Solzhenitsyn, Alexander. *One Day in the Life of Ivan Denisovich*.

Sontag, Susan. *In America*.

Spark, Muriel. *The Prime of Miss Jean Brodie*.

Stegner, Wallace. *Angle of Repose*.

Steinbeck, John. *East of Eden*.

Steinbeck, John. *The Grapes of Wrath*.

Steinbeck, John. *Of Mice and Men*.

Stendhal. *The Red and the Black*.

Stevenson, Robert Louis. *Dr. Jekyll and Mr. Hyde*.

Stoker, Bram. *Dracula*.

Stowe, Harriet Beecher. *Uncle Tom's Cabin*.

Styron, William. *The Confessions of Nat Turner*.

Styron, William. *Sophie's Choice*.

Swarthout, Glendon. *Bless the Beasts and the Children*.

Tan, Amy. *Joy Luck Club*.

Tanizaki, Junichiro. *Makioka Sisters*.

Thackeray, William. *Vanity Fair*.

Theroux, Paul. *The Mosquito Coast*.

Tolkien, J. R. R. *The Lord of the Rings*.

Tolstoy, Leo. *Anna Karenina*.

Tolstoy, Leo. *War and Peace*.

Toole, John K. *A Confederacy of Dunces*.

Traven, B. *The Treasure of the Sierra Madre*.

Tsao, Hsueh-chin. *The Dream of the Red Chamber*.

Turgenev, Ivan. *Fathers and Sons*.

Twain, Mark. *The Adventures of Huckleberry Finn*.

Twain, Mark. *The Adventures of Tom Sawyer*.

Tyler, Anne. *Breathing Lessons*.

Unset, Sigrid. *Kristin Lavransdatter*.

Updike, John. *Rabbit Run*.

Verne, Jules. *Twenty Thousand Leagues under the Sea*.

Vidal, Gore. *Lincoln*.

Voltaire. *Candide*.

Vonnegut, Kurt. *Slaughterhouse Five*.

Walker, Alice. *The Color Purple*.

Warren, Robert Penn. *All the King's Men*.

Waugh, Evelyn. *Brideshead Revisited*.

Welty, Eudora. *The Optimist's Daughter.*

Wharton, Edith. *Ethan Frome.*

Wharton, Edith. *The House of Mirth.*

White, T. H. *The Once and Future King.*

Wideman, John Edgar. *Fever: Twelve Stories.*

Wiesel, Elie. *Night.*

Wilde, Oscar. *The Picture of Dorian Gray.*

Wilder, Thornton. *The Bridge of San Luis Rey.*

Wolfe, Thomas. *Look Homeward, Angel.*

Wolfe, Tom. *Bonfire of the Vanities.*

Woolf, Virginia. *Mrs. Dalloway.*

Woolf, Virginia. *To the Lighthouse.*

Wouk, Herman. *War and Remembrance.*

Wouk, Herman. *The Winds of War.*

Wright, Richard. *Native Son.*

Zola, Emile. *Nana.*

SAMPLE MYSTERY CORE LIST
Criteria and Sources

The members of the mystery core committee are aware that there are many well-read mystery fans on staff and have taken their suggestions under advisement in developing this list of essential mysteries to be purchased by every agency in the Southwest Public Library system. It is with some trepidation that the mystery core committee presents its selections. Committee members, all of them mystery fans, strived to select those titles that met many of the following criteria:

1 | No more than two titles by one author

2 | Permanence and timelessness

3 | Originality and quality of writing

4 | Intrinsic quality when compared to other mysteries—titles that are significant to the genre

5 | Literary merit as expressed by reviewers

6 | Appearance of the title or author in the following special lists or bibliographies

> Breen, Jon L. *What about Murder? 1981–1991: A Guide to Books about Mystery and Detective Fiction.* Metuchen, N.J.: Scarecrow, 1993.

> Cox, J. Randolph. *Masters of Mystery and Detective Fiction: An Annotated Bibliography.* Pasadena, Calif.: Salem, 1989.

> Herald, Diana Tixier. *Genreflecting: A Guide to Reading Interests in Genre Fiction.* 6th ed. Englewood, Colo.: Libraries Unlimited, 2005.

Huang, Jim. *100 Favorite Mysteries of the Century.* Carmel, Ind.: Crum Creek, 2000. Titles were selected by the Independent Mystery Booksellers Association.

Mystery Writers of America. *Crown Crime Companion: The Top 100 Mystery Novels of All Time.* New York: Three River Press/Crown, 1995.

Niebuhr, Gary Warren. *Make Mine a Mystery: A Reader's Guide to Mystery and Detective Fiction.* Genreflecting Advisory Series. Englewood, Colo.: Libraries Unlimited, 2003.

Steinbrunner, Chris, and Otto Penzler. *Encyclopedia of Mystery and Detection.* New York: McGraw-Hill, 1976.

Winn, Dilys, comp. *Murder Ink: Revised, Revised, Still Unrepentant.* New York: Workman, 1984.

Winn, Dilys, comp. *Murderess Ink: The Better Half of the Mystery.* New York: Workman, 1979.

7 | Recipient of the Edgar Allan Poe Awards (the "Edgars"), which are given yearly by the Mystery Writers of America to the authors of distinguished work in various categories within the genre. Finalists can be located at www.mysterywriters.org, and previous winners and nominees in all categories at www.theedgars.com. The ALA Reading List Award, established in 2007 to highlight outstanding genre fiction, is a new source for core list additions. The winners are listed at www.ala.org.

8 | All core forum attendees are to follow these same criteria in recommending mysteries for the core collection.

Mystery Core List

Allingham, Margery. *Fashion in Shrouds.*

Block, Lawrence. *Dance at the Slaughter House.*

Cain, James. *The Postman Always Rings Twice.*

Chandler, Raymond. *The Big Sleep.*

Chesterton, G. K. *Innocence of Father Brown.*

Christie, Agatha. *The Murder of Roger Ackroyd.*

Christie, Agatha. *The Mysterious Affair at Styles.*

Cornwell, Patricia. *Postmortem.*

Cross, Amanda. *Death in a Tenured Position.*

Doyle, Sir Arthur Conan. *Complete Sherlock Holmes.*

Francis, Dick. *Dead Cert.*

Gardner, Erle Stanley. *Case of the Crooked Candle.*

Grafton, Sue. *A Is for Alibi.*

Hammett, Dashiell. *Maltese Falcon.*
Hiaasen, Carl. *Double Whammy.*
Highsmith, Patricia. *The Talented
Mr. Ripley.*
Hillerman, Tony. *Blessing Way.*
James, P. D. *Mr. White's
Confession.*
King, Laurie R. *Beekeeper's
Apprentice.*
Leonard, Elmore. *Killshot.*
MacDonald, John. *Dead Low Tide.*
MacDonald, Ross. *Drowning Pool.*

Marsh, Ngaio. *Wreath for Rivera.*
Mosley, Walter. *White Butterfly.*
Paretsky, Sara. *Bitter Medicine.*
Parker, Robert B., Jr. *Catskill Eagle.*
Peters, Ellis. *Morbid Taste for Bones.*
Priestley, J. B. *Salt Is Leaving.*
Rendell, Ruth. *New Lease on
Death.*
Sayers, Dorothy L. *Strong Poison.*
Stout, Rex. *Too Many Crooks.*
Tey, Josephine. *Singing Sands.*
Van Gulik, Robert. *Lacquer Screen.*

SAMPLE BIOGRAPHY CORE LIST
Criteria and Sources

The following statements should be considered in conjunction with Southwest Public Library's general core collection development policy statement. The core biography list should include only those titles that meet the following conditions:

1 | Accurate and thorough in research

2 | Readable and of current interest to the general public

3 | Objective and demonstrating honesty on the part of the author toward the subject

4 | Valid in terms of the author's credentials and qualifications

5 | Able to create an understanding of an individual's life or times

6 | Of literary merit as expressed by reviewers and appearance in important standard bibliographies

7 | Award winners or finalists for one of the following major awards [a description of these awards appears in chapter 6]:
   - Book Sense Book of the Year
   - National Book Award
   - National Book Critics' Circle Award
   - National Medal of the Arts
   - Nobel Prize
   - Pulitzer Prize

8 | A biography should *not* be included simply because the subject is important or is a popular cultural figure or because the author is

well known. For example, a president's biography will not be considered merely because the subject was the president.

9 | Every attempt will be made to include no more than two biographies of the same individual. However, in rare instances this limit may be waived if the titles are very different in perspective or deal with different portions of the subject's life.

10 | If the subject of the biography is an obscure person, but the book gives important insight into a particular time, place, or condition or the literary quality is extraordinary, it should be considered for core inclusion. For example: Anne Frank's *Diary of a Young Girl*, James Herriot's *All Creatures Great and Small*, or John Gunther's *Death Be Not Proud*.

Biography Core List

Adams, Ansel, and Mary S. Alinder. *Ansel Adams.*

Adams, Henry. *Education of Henry Adams.*

McCullough, David. *John Adams.*

Matleson, John. *Eden's Outcasts: The Story of Louisa May Alcott and Her Father.*

Angelou, Maya. *I Know Why the Caged Bird Sings.*

Bergreen, Laurence. *Louis Armstrong: An Extravagant Life.*

Rhodes, Richard. *John James Audubon: The Making of an American.*

Halperin, John. *Jane Austen.*

Weatherby, W. *James Baldwin: Artist on Fire.*

Garrett, Patrick. *Authentic Life of Billy the Kid.*

Faragher, John Mark. *Daniel Boone: The Life and Legend of an American Pioneer.*

Gaskell, Elizabeth. *Life of Charlotte Brontë.*

Clarke, Gerald. *Capote.*

Woodress, James. *Willa Cather: A Literary Life.*

Manchester, William. *Last Lion: Winston Spencer Churchill.*

Thurman, Judith. *Secrets of the Flesh: A Life of Colette.*

Morison, Samuel E. *Admiral of the Ocean Sea.*

Sewell, Richard. *Life of Emily Dickinson.*

Douglass, Frederick. *Narrative of the Life of Frederick Douglass, an American Slave.*

Huggins, Nathan Irvin. *Slave and Citizen: Life of Frederick Douglass.*

Baldwin, Neil. *Edison: Inventing the Century.*

Pais, Abraham. *Subtle Is the Lord: The Science and Life of Albert Einstein.*

Oates, Stephen B. *William Faulkner: The Man and the Artist.*

Turnbull, Andrew. *Scott Fitzgerald.*

Milford, Nancy. *Zelda.*

Green, Julian. *God's Fool: The Life of St. Francis of Assisi.*

Frank, Anne. *Diary of a Young Girl.*

Franklin, Benjamin. *Autobiography of Benjamin Franklin.*

Gay, Peter. *Freud: A Life for Our Time.*

Sobel, Dava. *Galileo's Daughter.*

Gandhi, Mahatma. *Gandhi's Autobiography: The Stories of My Experiments with Truth.*

Debo, Angie. *Geronimo: The Man, His Time, His Place.*

Gilbreth, Frank B., Jr., and Ernestine G. Carey. *Cheaper by the Dozen.*

van Gogh, Vincent. *Letters of Vincent van Gogh.*

Graham, Katherine. *Personal History.*

McFeely, William S. *Grant.*

Gunther, John. *Death Be Not Proud.*

Millgate, Michael. *Thomas Hardy.*

Baker, Carlos. *Ernest Hemingway: A Life Story.*

Herriot, James. *All Creatures Great and Small.*

Bix, Herbert P. *Hirohito and the Making of Modern Japan.*

Bullock, Alan. *Hitler: A Study in Tyranny.*

Hitler, Adolf. *Mein Kampf.*

Toland, John. *Adolf Hitler.*

Novick, Sheldon M. *Honorable Justice: The Life of Oliver Wendell Holmes.*

Rampersad, Arnold. *Life of Langston Hughes.*

Iacocca, Lee, and William Novak. *Iacocca.*

Meacham, Jon. *American Lion: Andrew Jackson in the White House.*

Remini, Robert V. *Andrew Jackson and the Course of American Democracy.*

Edel, Leon. *Henry James.*

Malone, Dumas. *Jefferson and His Time.*

Caro, Robert A. *Years of Lyndon Johnson: The Path to Power.*

Boswell, James. *Life of Samuel Johnson.*

Jung, Carl Gustav. *Memories, Dreams, Reflections.*

Keller, Helen. *The Story of My Life.*

Manchester, William. *Death of a President.*

Sorensen, Theodore C. *Kennedy.*

Schlesinger, Arthur. *Robert Kennedy and His Times.*

Collier, Peter, and David Horowitz. *Kennedys: An American Dream.*

Garrow, David J. *Bearing the Cross: Martin Luther King, Jr. and the Southern Christian Fellowship.*

Oates, Stephen B. *Let the Trumpet Sound: The Life of Martin Luther King, Jr.*

Kingston, Maxine Hong. *Woman Warrior.*

Freeman, Douglas Southall. *Lee.*

Landon, Margaret. *Anna and the King of Siam.*

Bishop, Jim. *The Day Lincoln Was Shot.*

Goodwin, Doris Kearns. *Team of Rivals: The Political Genius of Abraham Lincoln.*

Oates, Stephen. *With Malice towards None: The Life of Abraham Lincoln.*

Sandberg, Carl. *Abraham Lincoln: The Prairie Years and the War Years.*

Baker, Jean H. *Mary Todd Lincoln.*

Berg, A. Scott. *Lindbergh.*

Bainton, Roland H. *Here I Stand: A Life of Martin Luther.*

Manchester, William. *American Caesar: Douglas MacArthur.*

Meer, Fatima. *Higher Than Hope: A Biography of Nelson Mandela.*

Lovell, Mary S. *Straight on Till Morning: The Biography of Beryl Markham.*

Fraser, Antonia. *Mary, Queen of Scots.*

Mathabane, Mark. *Kaffir Boy.*

McCourt, Frank. *Angela's Ashes.*

Mead, Margaret. *Blackberry Winter.*

Solomon, Maynard. *Mozart.*

Schiff, Stacy. *Vera.*

Ambrose, Stephen E. *Nixon.*

Obama, Barack. *Dreams from My Father: A Story of Race and Inheritance.*

Massie, Robert K. *Peter the Great.*

Pirsig, Robert M. *Zen and the Art of Motorcycle Maintenance.*

Naifeh, Steven, and Gregory White Smith. *Jackson Pollock: An American Saga.*

Puller, Lewis B., Jr. *Fortunate Son: The Healing of a Vietnam Vet.*

Lash, Joseph R. *Eleanor and Franklin.*

McCullough, David G. *Mornings on Horseback.*

Morris, Edmund. *Rise of Theodore Roosevelt.*

Sarton, May. *At Seventy: A Journal.*

Schoenbaum, Samuel. *William Shakespeare.*

Brodie, Fawn M. *No Man Knows My History: The Life of Joseph Smith.*

Speer, Albert. *Inside the Third Reich.*

Deutscher, Isaac. *Stalin.*

Griffith, Elizabeth. *In Her Own Right: The Life of Elizabeth Cady Stanton.*

Stein, Gertrude. *Autobiography of Alice B. Toklas.*

Benson, Jackson J. *True Adventures of John Steinbeck, Writer.*

Hedrick, Joan D. *Harriet Beecher Stowe.*

Miller, Merle. *Plain Talking: An Oral History of Harry S. Truman.*

Kaplan, Justin. *Mr. Clemens and Mark Twain.*

Machado, Manuel A. *Centaur of the North: Francisco Villa, the Mexican Revolution and Northern Mexico.*

Washington, Booker T. *Up from Slavery.*

Flexner, James Thomas. *Washington: The Indispensable Man.*

Lewis, R. W. B. *Edith Wharton.*

Ellmann, Richard. *Oscar Wilde.*

Bell, Quentin. *Virginia Woolf.*

Twombly, Robert C. *Frank Lloyd Wright: His Life and His Architecture.*

Wright, Richard. *Black Boy.*

X, Malcolm. *Autobiography of Malcolm X.*

Arrington, Leonard J. *Brigham Young: American Moses.*

SAMPLE PHILOSOPHY CORE LIST
Criteria and Sources

Core titles in philosophy cover a range of thought from the very basic to the highly intellectual and include historic classics and the standard works by and about significant writers and thinkers. No attempt has been made to include all the great philosophers. Attention has been given to those works that exhibit the following qualities:

1 | Extraordinary literary merit

2 | Importance for an understanding of other literature in the humanities

3 | Value and continued significance to contemporary issues

4 | Original or unique subject treatment

5 | Interest and accessibility to the educated layperson

6 | Acknowledged merit, as shown by appearance in the bibliographies and checklists [outlined in chapter 6 of this volume], particularly the following titles:

- *Books for College Libraries*
- *Good Reading*
- *Living with Books*
- *Public Library Core Collection: Nonfiction*
- *The Reader's Adviser*
- *Reading Lists for College-Bound Students*

General library review sources do a good job of reviewing philosophy titles regularly. *Humanities Index* and *Philosophy Index* are resources for accessing reviews. Additionally, the following specialized journals review philosophy titles regularly:

- *Philosophical Books*
- *Philosophy Now*
- *Philosophy and Literature*
- *Philosophy East and West*
- *Teaching Philosophy*

Philosophy Core List

100	Descartes, Rene. *Principles of Philosophy.*
109	Durant, Will. *Story of Philosophy.*
109	Russell, Bertrand. *History of Western Philosophy.*
111	Sartre, Jean Paul. *Being and Nothingness.*

111.8	Adler, Mortimer. *Six Great Ideas.*
121	Locke, John. *Essay Concerning Human Understanding.*
121	Russell, Bertrand. *Inquiry into Meaning and Truth.*
131.34	Freud, Sigmund. *Basic Writings of Sigmund Freud.*
131.34	Hall, Calvin C. *Primer of Freudian Psychology.*
133	Wilson, Colin. *Occult.*
133.3	Stearn, Jess. *Edgar Cayce: Sleeping Prophet.*
133.32	Nostradamus. *Complete Prophecies.*
133.4	Leek, Sybil. *Complete Art of Witchcraft.*
133.4	Waite, Arthur Edward. *Book of Black Magic.*
133.5	Sakoian, Frances. *Astrologer's Handbook.*
133.8	McConnel, R. *Introduction to Parapsychology in the Context of Science.*
133.8	Rhine, Joseph B. *Extrasensory Perception.*
135.8	Freud, Sigmund. *The Interpretation of Dreams.*
136.1	May, Rollo. *Love and Will.*
136.2	Kübler-Ross, Elizabeth. *On Death and Dying.*
150	Carnegie, Dale. *How to Win Friends and Influence People.*
150	Kagan, Jerome. *Psychology.*
150	Skinner, B. F. *Science and Human Behavior.*
150	Watson, John B. *Behaviorism.*
150.19	Rogers, Carl R. *Way of Being.*
150.19	Skinner, B. F. *Beyond Freedom and Dignity.*
150.195	Frankel, Victor. *Man's Search for Meaning.*
150.195	Jung, C. G. *Essential Jung.*
150.922	Watson, Robert. *Great Psychologists.*
153.930	Gould, Stephen Jay. *Mismeasure of Man.*
154.4	Gladwell, Malcolm. *Blink: The Power of Thinking without Thinking.*
154.4	Leary, Timothy. *Politics of Ecstasy.*
155.232	Lasswell, Harold D. *Power and Personality.*
155.422	Klaus, Marshall H. *Amazing Newborn.*
155.916	Beattie, Melodie. *Codependent No More.*
155.937	Lifton, Robert Jay. *Broken Connection.*
158.1	James, Muriel, and Dorothy Jongeward. *Born to Win.*
158.2	Buscaglia, Leo. *Love.*
158.24	Friday, Nancy. *My Mother, Myself.*
160	Kant, Immanuel. *Introduction to Logic.*
179	Tillich, Paul. *Courage to Be.*
181.1	Confucius. *Wisdom of Confucius.*
181.3	Buber, Martin. *I and Thou.*
184	Plato. *Dialogues.*
185	Aristotle. *Basic Works.*
190	Critchley, Simon. *Book of Dead Philosophers.*
193	Nietzsche, Friedrich. *Thus Spake Zarathustra.*

SAMPLE RELIGION CORE LIST
Criteria and Sources

The Southwest Public Library recognizes that religion is an integral part of human life and that the library's users participate in many different religions, denominations, and sects. The religion core collection is intended for use by general readers whatever their denomination and inclination. The purpose of the religion core collection is to provide basic knowledge and promote understanding of the major religions of the world by providing works of the highest literary merit, authority, and timelessness.

The collection is not intended for the pursuit of personal religious interests. The library is a supporter of no one religion, sect, or cult. At all times it must be remembered that the library is an educational institution and not a religious agency. Core selection is broad, tolerant, and without partisanship or propaganda and always geared toward choosing the best material. No attempt is made to provide a balanced core collection in religion; this is the responsibility of the general collection. To avoid personal bias of any kind, local experts will be asked to review core selection lists before their distribution for selection.

In addition to the policy outlined in the core selection development policy, core religion selectors select titles that include the following:

1 | Sacred texts of the major religions

2 | Representation of the most important spokespersons of the major religions

3 | Books reviewed as "indispensable" by scholarly journals

4 | Landmark studies

5 | Award winners or titles that appear in the major bibliographic resources for public libraries

6 | Critically acclaimed or favorably reviewed titles in popular magazines geared to the general public

Although there are numerous magazines written for specific denominations and selectors might wish to look at these, core titles most likely come from standard review media that are written for the information-seeking lay member of the general public and not for divinity students or those proselytizing one faith. A good specialized source to keep abreast of newly published general religion titles is *Publishers Weekly Religion BookLine,* a weekly online newsletter also available as a subscription. *BookLine* is geared for the religion professional, with short prepublication reviews of academic reference books and religion and spirituality titles. It also includes informative articles on trends in religion books, author interviews, and publishing news.

Religion Core List

200.9	Armstrong, Karen. *Battle for God.*
209.73	Ahlstrom, S. E. *Religious History of the American People.*
220.15	Lindsey, Hal. *Late Great Planet Earth.*
220.52	Revised English Bible with Apocrypha.
220.520	Holy Bible (King James Version).
220.520	Strong, James. *New Strong's Exhaustive Concordance of the Bible.*
220.520	New American Bible (St. Joseph's edition)
220.520	Good News Bible.
220.527	New Jerusalem Bible.
220.7	Brown, Raymond E. *New Jerome Biblical Commentary.*
221.4	Vermes, Goza. *Dead Sea Scrolls in English.*
222.107	Plaut, W. Gunther. *The Torah: A Modern Commentary.*
225.5	Phillips, J. B. *New Testament in Modern English.*
226.2	Bonhoeffer, Dietrich. *Cost of Discipleship.*
229	Metzger, Bruce Manning. *Introduction to the Apocrypha.*
230	Lewis, C. S. *Mere Christianity.*
230.09	Tillich, Paul. *A History of Christian Thought.*
230.2	Rahner, Karl. *Foundations of Christian Faith.*
231	Miles, Jack. *God: A Biography.*
231.7	Niebuhr, H. Richard. *The Meaning of Revelation.*
231.73	Lewis, C. S. *Miracles: A Preliminary Study.*
236.24	Bounds, Edward McKendree. *Heaven: A Place, a City, a Home.*
237	Moody, Richard. *Life after Life.*
242	Augustine, Saint. *Confessions of St. Augustine.*
242.1	Thomas à Kempis. *Imitation of Christ.*
248.4	Lewis, C. S. *Screwtape Letters.*
248.4	Peale, Norman Vincent. *The Power of Positive Thinking.*
248.482	Merton, Thomas. *No Man Is an Island.*
255	Norris, Kathleen. *Cloister Walk.*
259.509	Wilkerson, David R. *Cross and the Switch Blade.*
270	Latourette, Kenneth Scott. *History of Christianity.*
272	Foxe, John. *Foxe's Book of Martyrs.*
282.092	Walsh, Michael. *Butler's Lives of the Saints.*
282.73	Ellis, John Tracy. *American Catholicism.*
289.3	Shipps, Jan. *Mormonism.*
289.3	Smith, Joseph. *Doctrine and Covenants of the Church of Jesus Christ of Latter Day Saints.*
289.322	Book of Mormon.
289.92	Eddy, Mary Baker. *Science and Health.*
289.92	Penton, M. James. *Apocalypse Delayed: The Story of Jehovah's Witnesses.*

290	Hamilton, Edith. *Mythology.*
291	Frazer, James. *The New Golden Bough.*
291	Gibran, Kahlil. *The Prophet.*
291	Smith, Huston. *World's Religions.*
291.097	Gaustad, Edwin Scott. *Religious History of America.*
291.097	Hudson, Winthrop. *Religion in America.*
291.13	Bulfinch, Thomas. *Bulfinch's Mythology.*
291.13	Campbell, Joseph. *Masks of God.*
291.42	James, William. *Varieties of Religious Experience.*
291.82	Smart, Ninian, and Richard Hecht. *Sacred Texts of the World.*
292.13	Graves, Robert. *Greek Myths.*
294.3	Suzuki, Daisetz T. *Essentials of Zen Buddhism.*
294.342	Sogyal Rinpoche. *Tibetan Book of Living and Dying.*
294.392	Watts, Alan. *Spirit of Zen.*
294.592	Murthy, B. Srinivasa. *Bhagavad Gita.*
296	Heschel, Abraham J. *God in Search of Man.*
296.1	Holtz, Barry W., ed. *Back to the Sources: Reading the Classic Jewish Texts.*
296.12	Cohen, Abraham. *Everyman's Talmud.*
296.833	Scholem, Gershoma. *Major Trends in Jewish Mysticism.*
297	Esposito, John L. *Islam: The Straight Path.*
297.122	Holy Qur'an.
297.122	Arberry, Arthur J. *Koran Interpreted.*
299.31	Ancient Egyptian Book of the Dead.
299.514	Lao-Tzu. *Tao Te Ching.*
299.59	Bhagavad Gita.
299.7	Castaneda, Carlos. *Teachings of Don Juan.*
299.93	Adler, Margot. *Drawing Down the Moon: Witches, Druids, Goddess Worshippers.*
299.93	Gil, Sam D. *Native American Religions.*

SAMPLE NATURAL SCIENCES CORE LIST
Criteria and Sources

The Southwest Public Library recognizes that there is considerable interest in the natural sciences. The subject of natural science has an unusual lasting value for two reasons. First, natural science is a systematic discipline: data are collected, hypotheses are derived from observations, and theories are evolved that correlate and explain that which is known. Therefore, the history and development of the sciences, even the abandoned byways, are important to an understanding of where we are today. Second, the ongoing rapid changes in our environment make the record of floras and faunas and of endangered species particularly important to an understanding of where we are going. Core selection must be done with an eye to the past as well as the future. Books must appeal to the interested nonspecialist. The essential core selection criterion for choosing one natural science book over another is that the quality of writing be as good as the science.

Natural science selection is performed as outlined in the Southwest Public Library's core collection policy statement. In addition to the standard library review media, there are several excellent science magazines appropriate for the general reader that regularly review science books or include articles by the best writers in the field. These magazines include but are not limited to *Audubon, Discover, Environment, National Geographic, Natural History, Nature, New Scientist, Popular Science, Science, Scientific American,* and *Smithsonian.* Additionally, *Science Books and Films,* published online by the American Association for the Advancement of Science, is an excellent critical review source for science books that appeal to the general reader. There are numerous indexes that provide access to science periodicals, such as General Sciences Abstracts and Applied Science and Technology Abstracts. The National Association of Science Writers gives one book yearly its Science in Society Award for outstanding reporting about the sciences and their impact on society good or bad, and particularly to a book that did not receive an award from a special interest group. A list of these winners is at www.nasw.org.

Natural Sciences Core List

501	Bronowski, Jacob. *Ascent of Man.*
508	Darwin, Charles. *Voyage of the Beagle.*
510.1	Hofstader, Douglas. *Godel, Escher, Bach.*
510.9	Boyer, Carl B. *History of Mathematics.*
523	Pasachoff, Jay, and Donald H. Menzel. *Field Guide to the Stars and Planets.*
523.1	Hawking, Stephen. *Brief History of Time.*
526.62	Sobel, Dava. *Longitude.*
530.11	Einstein, Albert. *Meaning of Relativity.*
531	Newton, Isaac. *Mathematical Principles of Natural Philosophy.*
539.7	Close, Frank E. *Particle Explosion.*
548	Holden, Alan. *Crystals and Crystal Growing.*
549.1	Pough, Frederick H. *Field Guide to Rocks and Minerals.*
551.46	Carson, Rachel L. *The Sea around Us.*
557.3	McPhee, John A. *Annals of the Former World.*
565.39	Fortey, Richard. *Trilobite!*
567.91	Bakker, Robert T. *Dinosaur Heresies.*
567.91	Lambert, David. *Field Guide to Dinosaurs.*
569.9	Johanson, Donald. *Lucy.*
572.86	Watson, James. *Double Helix.*
573.3	Leakey, Richard E. *Origins.*

574	Attenborough, David. *Living Planet.*
574.92	Cousteau, Jacques Yves. *The Ocean World.*
575	Attenborough, David. *Life on Earth.*
575	Gould, Stephen Jay. *Ever since Darwin.*
575	Margulis, Lyn. *Microcosmos.*
575.01	Darwin, Charles. *On the Origin of Species.*
576.82	Jones, Steve. *Darwin's Ghost.*
577	Burdick, Alan. *Out of Eden.*
577	Thomas, Lewis. *Lives of a Cell.*
581.632	Gibbons, Euell. *Stalking the Wild Asparagus.*
591.04	Ehrlich, Paul R. *Extinction.*
591.5	Lorenz, Konrad. *On Aggression.*
591.51	Masson, J. Moussaieff. *When Elephants Weep.*
595.79	Holldobler, Bert, and Edward O. Wilson. *The Ants.*
598.2	Audubon, James. *Birds of America.*
598.29	Peterson, Roger Tory. *Field Guide to Birds.*
598.29	Sibley, David. *Sibley Guide to Birds.*
598.883	Weiner, Jonathan. *Beak of the Finch.*
599.53	Lilly, John C. *Communication between Man and Dolphin.*
599.744	Adamson, Joy. *Born Free.*
599.744	Lopez, Barry Holstun. *Of Wolves and Men.*
599.744	Mowat, Farley. *Never Cry Wolf.*
599.744	Schaller, George B. *Last Panda.*
599.744	Schaller, George B. *Serengeti Lion.*
599.744	Thomas, Elizabeth. *Hidden Lives of Dogs.*
599.8	Goodall, Jane. *In the Shadow of Man.*
599.9	Olson, Steve. *Mapping Human History.*
599.98	Fossey, Dian. *Gorillas in the Mist.*

SAMPLE FILM CORE LIST
Criteria and Sources

The emphasis of the Southwest Public Library's core film collection is to obtain only the most critically acclaimed feature films available for home use. Foreign films that have won a major award in their countries or that meet the criteria outlined below are also selected. Foreign films are excellent resources for learning about diverse cultures. The subtitled version of a foreign film will always be purchased in order to retain the integrity of the movie.

Although the medium of film has been around only for a little over a hundred years, the advent of the movie rental business has resulted in several critical guides to feature films. The movie review media and film awards are quite extensive, providing a surprising number of excellent resources for core film selection.

The following core criteria were developed for core film collection development and should be considered in conjunction with the general core criteria as outlined in the Southwest Public Library's core collection development policy statement:

1 | Films that have won one or more of the following major awards or association or festival honorable mentions:

- Academy Award
- BAFTA Award (British Academy of Film and Television Arts)
- Broadcast Film Critics Association
- Cannes Film Festival Awards
- Directors Guild of America
- Film Critics Award
- Golden Bear (Berlin Film Festival award)
- Golden Globe
- Independent Spirit Award
- Los Angeles Film Critics Circle Awards
- National Board of Review
- National Society of Film Critics
- New York Film Critics Circle
- Online Film Critics Society Awards
- SAG Award (Screen Actors Guild)
- Sundance Film Festival Award
- Toronto Film Festival Award
- Writers Guild of America Awards

2 | Films that have been included in the following prestigious lists:

- All-TIME 100 Movies
- American Film Institute's list of America's 100 Greatest Movies
- British Film Institute List
- Library of Congress's National Film Registry
- TV Guide's 50 Greatest Movies on TV and Video

3 | Classic films that were produced at least twenty years ago and have proved of long-term or lasting value. These films should appear in most books on film study and should exemplify the very best of filmmaking and illustrate the history and development of film as an art form. They may be purchased even though they do not meet the latest technological standards for picture quality and sound. Colorized (changed from their original black-and-white format) or dubbed films will not be purchased.

4 | Films that were produced within the past six to twenty years and have over the course of time gained in importance so that they

regularly appear in cinematography texts and "best of" lists shall be considered.

5 | Although it is impossible to judge whether a newly released film (within the past five years) will eventually be considered a classic, it can be purchased for the core collection if it meets the following rigorous standards:

  a. The film has won one of the major awards listed earlier.

  b. A feature film has at least three excellent reviews by leading film critics.

  c. The film must, in the opinion of the selector, be of outstanding merit and importance in the study of film or society.

  d. Additionally, it is recommended that the selector view the film in its entirety before core selection.

6 | Films that are examples of the work of the most important and acclaimed directors will be considered.

7 | All core film selections should appear in the following film guides and have received an excellent review or four-star rating:

  Classic Movie Companion. Edited by Robert Moses for AMC (American Movie Classics). New York: Hyperion, 1999. Concise reviews of American movie classics.

  Halliwell's Film Guide 2004. 19th ed. Edited by John Walker. New York: HarperCollins, 2003. Highly respected and sharply opinionated reviews edited, since Leslie Halliwell died in 1989, by one of Britain's leading film experts. Excellent coverage of non-American films.

  "Have You Seen . . . ?" A Personal Introduction to 1000 Films. By David Thomson. New York: Knopf, 2008. One of the most influential film critics today, Thomson compiles his personal list of the one thousand must-see films to help answer the question he is often asked: "What should I see?" His evaluations are informative and witty and are arranged alphabetically with an accompanying chronological index.

  Leonard Maltin's Classic Movie Guide. By Leonard Maltin. New York: Penguin Group, 2005. Esteemed film historian and author of the annual *Movie Guide,* listed below, presents his authoritative guide to classic movies along with his unique top ten lists.

Leonard Maltin's Movie 2009 Guide. Edited by Leonard
Maltin. New York: New American Library, 2009. Written by one of the country's most respected film historians
and a member of the National Film Preservation Board,
which selects the twenty-five films named each year to the
Library of Congress's National Film Registry. Concise critical reviews, with movies rated from four stars to "bomb."
Updated yearly.

Movie Awards. Rev. ed. Edited by Tom O'Neil. New York:
Penguin Group, 2003. Compares the major film awards
and lists many of the association award winners, including
Golden Globe, Critics Guild, SGA, Screen Actors, Directors, Writers, and Producers guilds of America awards.

New York Times Guide to the Best 1,000 Movies Ever Made.
Rev. ed. By the film critics of the *New York Times.* New
York: Random House, 2004. Original reviews from the
New York Times written by its esteemed film critics.

Roger Ebert's Four-Star Reviews, 1967–2007. Kansas City,
Mo.: Andrews McNeel, 2007. Includes all of Pulitzer
Prize–winning film critic Ebert's four-star reviews.

Time Out Film Guide, 2009. 17th ed. Edited by John Pym.
London: Time Out Group, 2009. Critical reviews con-
densed from *Time Out* magazine, London's premier
weekly guide to cultural events throughout the city.
Includes many international films along with the chief
prize winners of the BAFTA and the film festivals of
Cannes and Venice. A directory of film-related websites is
included along with a list of one hundred keynote films
from the history of cinema.

Additional Sources

Craddock, Jim, ed. *VideoHound's Golden Movie Retriever, 2009.* Florence,
Ky.: Gale Cengage 2008.
Capsule reviews with ratings of "no bones" to "4 bones." Ratings are not as critical as in the previous sources, and movies are evaluated on their appropriateness
for family viewing. Includes in-depth indexes to actors and directors.

Gilmour, David. *Film Club: A Memoir.* New York: Twelve Books, 2009.
Canadian film critic and novelist Gilmour tells of his decision to let his teen-
age son drop out of high school if he agrees to watch three films a week with

him. This is a touching look at the trials of being a dad and the therapeutic powers of movies. Gilmour certainly makes a strong case for the importance of films. His accompanying list of the movies they watched together provides an excellent start for core film collections.

Martin, Mick, and Marsha Porter. *DVD and Video Guide 2007*. New York: Ballantine, 2006.
Concise summaries rated from five stars to "turkey." Useful indexes of cast members and directors and an alternative title index, all of which can help you locate a movie.

Mowrey, Peter C. *Award Winning Films: A Viewer's Reference to 2700 Acclaimed Motion Pictures*. Jefferson, N.C.: McFarland, 1994.
Essentially one person's opinion of what he considers the best films, "cream of the crop." Critical film reviews are listed with awards won for each movie. Appendix of the 204 most award-winning movies of all time.

Variety's Film Reviews. New Providence, N.J.: R. R. Bowker, since 1907.
Complete reproduction of the actual full-text feature film reviews from *Variety*, arranged chronologically by review publication date. Film title and director index included.

Wilhelm, Eliot. *VideoHound's World Cinema: The Adventurer's Guide to Movie Watching*. Detroit, Mich.: Visible Ink, 1999.
Primarily international in scope with critical reviews including suggestions for additional viewings. Sidebars throughout book about internationally acclaimed directors.

Movie-Related Websites on Classic Films

American Film Institute, www.afionline.org. Covers AFI 100 Greatest Films, with features on classic films.

American Movie Classics, www.amctv.com. AMC's site has articles on classic movies and filmographies, including resources for film purchase.

AMC Filmsite, www.filmsite.org. Provides detailed plot summaries, reviews, and analysis of the great movies of the past century.

Movie Review Query Engine, www.mrqe.com. The leading online index of movie reviews provides easy access to all published and available reviews.

Rotten Tomatoes, www.rottentomatoes.com. Devoted to reviews, information, and movie news, this entertaining website gives readers a one-glance overview of the critical opinions of a film through its tomato icons. Positive "fresh" reviews receive a red tomato, negative "rotten" ones a green splatted tomato. The separate Top Critics listing is particularly helpful.

UCLA Film and Television Archive, www.cinema.ucla.edu. Includes lists of best films and background on studios and directors.

Variety magazine, www.variety.com. Trade magazine available online and as a weekly newspaper that offers broad coverage of movies, theater, and music. Written for the trade, but a good way to keep up with reviews, trends, and technology in the entertainment industry.

Video Librarian, www.videolibrarian.com. Provides free access to classic film reviews and new movie reviews. The bimonthly print magazine is written for public, school, and academic libraries with over two hundred reviews and articles on video-related news and technological trends. Video Librarian Plus! combines the print subscription with online access to a database of full-text reviews.

Film Core List

The Adventures of Robin Hood (1938)
The African Queen
All about Eve
All Quiet on the Western Front
Amadeus
American Beauty
American Graffiti
And Then There Were None
Annie Hall
Apocalypse Now
Ashes and Diamonds
Au Revoir, Les Enfants
Battleship Potemkin
Ben Hur
The Birth of a Nation
Blue Angel
Braveheart
Breaker Morant
The Bridge on the River Kwai
Broadway Melody
The Cabinet of Dr. Caligari

Casablanca
Cat on a Hot Tin Roof
Chinatown
Citizen Kane
City Lights
A Clockwork Orange
Close Encounters of the Third Kind
The Color Purple
Crouching Tiger, Hidden Dragon
Dances with Wolves
The Deer Hunter
Do the Right Thing
Double Indemnity
Dr. Strangelove
Duck Soup
Easy Rider
8½
El Norte
The English Patient
Fanny and Alexander
Fantasia

Farewell My Concubine
Fargo
The Four Horsemen of the
  Apocalypse
400 Blows
The French Connection
Gallipoli
Gandhi
General
Gentleman's Agreement
The Godfather
The Godfather Part II
Gone with the Wind
Goodfellas
The Graduate
Grand Hotel
The Grand Illusion
The Grapes of Wrath
The Great Train Robbery
The Great Ziegfeld
Hamlet (1948)
High Noon
The Hunchback of Notre Dame
  (1923)
I Am a Fugitive from a Chain Gang
In the Heat of the Night
It Happened One Night
It's a Wonderful Life
The Jazz Singer
King Kong (1933)
La Dolce Vita
The Last Emperor
Lawrence of Arabia
The Lord of the Rings: The
  Fellowship of the Ring
M*A*S*H
A Man for All Seasons
The Manchurian Candidate (1962)
The Mark of Zorro (1920)
Marty
Midnight Cowboy
Mr. Smith Goes to Washington

Mrs. Miniver
Mutiny on the Bounty (1935)
My Fair Lady
Nanook of the North
On the Waterfront
One Flew over the Cuckoo's Nest
Patton
Pelle the Conqueror
Persona
Platoon
Psycho (1960)
Pulp Fiction
Raging Bull
Rebel without a Cause
Schindler's List
Seven Beauties
Seven Samurai
Shakespeare in Love
Shane
The Silence of the Lambs
Singin' in the Rain
Snow White and the Seven Dwarfs
Some Like It Hot
The Sound of Music
Spirited Away
Star Wars Episode IV: A New Hope
A Streetcar Named Desire
Taxi Driver
The Ten Commandments (1956)
The Thief of Bagdad (1940)
The Third Man
To Kill a Mockingbird
Traffic
2001: A Space Odyssey
Unforgiven (1992)
West Side Story
Who's Afraid of Virginia Woolf?
The Wild Bunch
The Wizard of Oz
The World of Apu
Yankee Doodle Dandy
Z

Note: Authors, titles, and subjects are interfiled in one index. Authors appear in roman, titles in italics, and subjects in boldface.

You may also be interested in

Fundamentals of Collection Development and Management, Second Edition: Johnson offers a comprehensive tour of this essential discipline and situates the fundamental ideas of collection development and management in historical and theoretical perspective, bringing this modern classic fully up to date.

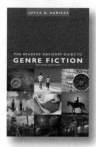

The Readers' Advisory Handbook: Covering everything from getting to know a library's materials to marketing and promoting readers' advisory, this practical handbook will help you expand services immediately without adding costs or training time.

The Readers' Advisory Guide to Genre Fiction, Second Edition: Provocative and spirited, this new edition offers hands-on strategies for librarians who want to become experts at figuring out what their readers are seeking and how to match books with those interests.

The Newbery and Caldecott Awards, 2010 Edition: Newly updated to include all 2010 award winners, the latest edition of the Newbery and Caldecott Awards guide covers the most distinguished American children's literature and illustration.

Order today at www.alastore.ala.org or 866-746-7252!